Suffer Well

Walking Victoriously Through Your Valleys

Dan Herod

Speak It To Book
www.speakittobook.com

Suffer Well / Dan Herod
ISBN-13: 978-1-945793-39-4
ISBN-10: 1-945793-39-2

In *Suffer Well*, Dan Herod invites you in—transparently and openly—as he and his family journey through one of the darkest challenges one could face. However, Dan's story and the hope that he shares do not end in despair, and it need not end in despair for you or me, either. Too often we suffer in silence, or we are paralyzed by not knowing where to start in processing painful life events. Dan shatters the silence with a fresh, positive, and biblical perspective. I am so grateful to call Dan and Marlena my friends. Dan extends an invitation of friendship to you in this book with honesty, encouragement, and wisdom so we all can learn how to suffer well.

—Kent Hulbert, National Youth Alive® Missionary

When it comes to suffering and surviving the trials of life, there is no one better on the topic than Dan Herod. This isn't a topic he's researched; it's something he and his family have lived through. If you are going through a hard time, you have lived through loss, or you're just a human being who has to go through difficulty at some point, then this is the book you need to read.

—Terrence Talley, author of *Our Story*
   www.TerrenceTalley.com

Few have walked the road of suffering Dan has, but the truth is we all will. Your details are different, but our pain is the same. That said, you will need a guide. Dan shows you the way to suffer well. It's possible in your impossible. His life is the smoking gun to that truth.

—**Eric Samuel Timm**
   Orator, artist, author of *Static Jedi* (latest release)
   www.EricSamuelTimm.com

"Thank you" fails to effectively capture the depth of my gratitude as I think about everyone who helped me get this far. Until I find another way to say it, however, it will suffice.

I owe the world to the One who spoke the world into existence. God's faithful love in my life has made me who I am today. Without His presence I would be a different person, in a different place, doing very different things. I surely would not have written this book.

To my amazing bride and partner in crime, Marlena: You are the epitome of grace. Your love for others grabbed my attention many years ago and has held it ever since. You are more than beautiful. You are faithful, thoughtful, and wonderful in so many ways. We never knew our life together would twist and turn the way it did. With poise, you have taken every punch life has thrown at us. With fire in your soul, you have risen to your feet with me every time we were knocked down. You make me want to be a better man, husband, father, and follower of Jesus. Thank you, Cutie.

To my in-laws, Beth and Thom: The way you two selflessly give to everyone around you inspires me to do the same. Your support is unrelenting. Your love is sacrificial. Your strength is steadfast. You never expect anything in return. You both have shown me what Jesus would do in so many moments. Thank you.

To our friends Dan and Theresa: You will never know how much you added to our journey. The countless hours spent on the phone, combined with the many meals our families have shared, enriched us deeply. Dan, I still think your 'Putin on a Ritz' joke isn't funny. Even so, thank you.

To the Tangeman family: Your friendship and support over the years has never wavered. We cannot say enough when we consider how you expressed your love for our family. Thank you.

To Pastor Dave and Julie: You gave us a shot to serve in ministry alongside you many years ago. Serving with you was a true privilege. The faithful friendship we maintain to this day is invaluable. Thank you.

To Steve and Kristie: Your leadership in our lives was a catalyst for many good things. Your friendship fostered even more. You walked with us through our darkest days—and still do. You always care more about who we are than what we do. Thank you.

To our family: Your love and support through our most difficult season of life have never wavered. I am grateful to be on this journey with you all. Thank you.

To my unofficial editor, Jacob: Your insight into authorship is compelling. Your honest feedback was timely and catalytic. Thank you.

To the official editors, artists, and workbook creators at Speak It To Book: The way you took my manuscript to a professional level is amazing. I am grateful for all of your hard work. Thank you.

To my angel investor, Andria: Your willingness to give financially toward this book in the midst of your own season of suffering is inspirational. Thank you.

To the countless others in my life who encouraged me to write this book: Thank you!

CONTENTS

Life

My lungs were burning. The crisp autumn air ignited my heaving chest as it begged for oxygen. I began to wonder: *Will this race ever end?*

When I was in high school, I ran cross country for one season. Why on God's green earth did I sign up for a sport like that? Running is hard! If you do it right, all you want to do is stop. I am only half-joking, folks.

Your heart pounds and your whole body cries tears of pain. Most people call this sweating. If you're lucky, the beads of sweat will miss your eyes as they travel down your forehead and off the tip of your nose. If you're normal, you will spend the entirety of your run trying to blink away the stinging sensation your sweat is authoring for you. While suffering does not necessarily mean that you are running, running most certainly means that you are suffering to some degree.

While I still have no idea why I decided to run cross-country that year, it wasn't all bad. One of my favorite races we did was in Duluth, Minnesota. It was called the

Swain Cross Country Invitational. Swain has been running every fall since 1951. This race boasts a challenging three-mile course and draws teams from all over the region.

The leaves were changing color the year I ran it. I will never forget when my cross-country team approached the outskirts of Duluth on our coach bus. While my face wasn't necessarily pressed up against the window next to my seat, I was struck by the intense beauty that welcomed me to town. The picturesque scene rolled up and down endless hills surrounding the city. Beautiful browns, yellows, and greens fused into a masterpiece collage that took my breath away.

The large coach bus came to a clean stop at the race course, and my teammates and I exited with great anticipation. We completed our pre-race preparations and headed to the starting line. It was time to do what we came to do.

I stood on the starting line before the race began, with runners to my right and left. Towering before me was the hill that we would climb. Yes, you read that right. This race started in a valley. Imagine running across a soccer field that tilted up. Going down would be easy. Running up it would be a grind to say the least.

With one crisp blast, the starting gun announced the beginning of the race. The sound of my shoes pounding the grass adding to the deafening rumble created by the crush of runners all around me. My ascent out of the valley had begun.

I ran up that hill to start the race. I ran it again in the middle of the race. I ran up it one last time to cross the finish line. Ascending out of the valley three times led me to be believe that it was most assuredly one hill of a race! Each of the three miles had a valley to overcome.

Each time I approached the valley, a sense of dread filled my entire being as I knew the difficulty ahead. Running out of the valley was physically, mentally, and emotionally exhausting. Everything in me wanted to collapse in defeat.

If I am being honest, discouragement hit me hard as I raced out of the valley for the second time. My legs ached, and my lungs burned. My arms felt like sandbags attached to my shoulders. My body desperately wanted me to quit my race every time I encountered a valley. I couldn't possibly go on. But I did, and I finished the race.

I am proud of what I accomplished that day I crossed the finish line because I kept running through the suffering. In other words, I suffered well.

Life can be a lot like my cross-country race in Duluth. Some stretches of life are so beautiful that they take your breath away. Other parts are so difficult that you can barely breathe. When you experience a valley, or a hard time in life, it is a season of suffering that begs you to despair—to lose hope. How you suffer unveils the substance of your relationship with God.

This race is real, and God wants you to win. How we run through every season is important. However, the way we navigate the valleys of life have a profound impact. The way we journey through difficult seasons will shape our lives for years to come.

I am convinced that our western view of Jesus is polluted by our prosperity. I say this because countless individuals with faith in Jesus are shocked when they suffer in any way, shape or form. The theological assumption is that they must be doing something wrong, or worse, that God is punishing them.

If we are to experience the fullness of Jesus' message, we must make room for the broad spectrum of suffering that comes with the human experience. We can no longer afford to ignore the glaring truth that we will suffer many things on this side of eternity. Loss, hardship, persecution, disease, dysfunction, and death are all part of life. But Jesus is not a stranger to suffering, and He walks with us through it all.

It is time to open our eyes to all that faith in Jesus involves. It is a race that is full of struggle, hard decisions, and sacrifice. To finish well, you must suffer well. God intentionally uses the metaphor of running to help us understand how He sees life. Read the following verses from the book of Hebrews:

> *Therefore, since we are surrounded by such a great cloud of witnesses, let us throw off everything that hinders and the sin that so easily entangles. And let us run with perseverance the race marked out for us, fixing our eyes on Jesus, the pioneer and perfecter of faith. For the joy set before him he endured the cross, scorning its shame, and sat down at the right hand of the throne of God.*
> **—Hebrews 12:1-2** (NIV)

God wants you to know that you are not alone. As you run your race, you are surrounded by the entire family of faith. They watch you now from heaven and here on earth. Everyone wants you to finish. To finish well you must suffer well. To suffer well, you must learn how to conquer the valleys in life.

Valleys can make or break you. These seasons of suffering introduce us to the cold reality that life is not fair. It never has been. It never will be. While the unfairness of life is a bitter pill, the presence of God in it all is breath for our lungs. He is good when life is not.

You may be in a valley right now where the difficulty you face is more than you can handle. You may have a friend who needs you to walk through their painful valley with them. You may be watching someone journey through their valley from a distance.

Whether you are the sufferer, supporter, or spectator, it is important to remember that simple math can save the day in seasons of suffering:

God's Presence + Your Faith Response = Abundant Life

The equation is elementary, and the outcome is empowering.

The first part of the equation is God. His presence in every valley provides power to overcome. God is exponential in nature, and He produces outcomes that are impossible without Him.

The second part of the equation is you. Your response to the difficulty that surrounds you determines what happens in you. Your faith response in life's darkest valleys cannot be overstated. Will you make wise or unwise decisions in response to the pain? When your faith in God enters the equation, abundant life is the result. The choice is yours.

When God's presence meets your faith response, an exponential explosion takes place in the valley. Regardless of the circumstance, the outcome is always abundant life.

Jesus gives every suffering soul the promise of abundant life through the valley. There is an adversary who seeks to take from us. Jesus makes it crystal clear that He came to give in the following Bible verse:

> *The thief comes only to steal and kill and destroy. I came that they may have life and have it abundantly.*
> *—John 10:10 (ESV)*

The beauty of this promise is the fact that we can trust the One who said it. It does not come with conditions that depend on circumstances. Jesus is the life giver in every season, outside the valley and in it. Seasons of suffering will bring you to your knees in agony. Even then, we have a say in how we respond to the darkest of days. Jesus showed us the way to walk. He endured the unfathomable to offer us the unbelievable.

It is my goal in this book to change the way we talk about suffering. That men, women, boys and girls would bravely embrace the reality that life will not be easy and the call of the cross is radically counter-cultural. We must reject the notion that Jesus came to make life easy.

My friend Eric Samuel Timm is a renowned orator, artist, and author. He says it this way: "Jesus didn't come to make life easy; He came to make life possible." One look into God's word and we discover that is exactly what He came to do.

This book is meant to be a journey. I share my deepest pain that is born out of loss. I invite you into my story because I want to help you live abundantly in your story.

The intensity of the valley in the Swain race is a continual reminder to me that in this life we will have suffering. In fact, in each of our lives we will experience our own variation of the "Three Mile Valley"—a metaphorical place intended to represent our literal path through life's darkest days.

Reflecting on the race I ran that day in Duluth, I can't help but see how that race represents something that each and every one of us encounters in life: suffering. The race was just over three miles long, with each mile being different than the others. Every single mile was unique because of its terrain. It is almost like the terrain was my teacher and I was the student. Although it felt more like a test, it was actually my classroom. The terrain was instructive as it unpacked a key lesson that I will carry with me for the rest of my life: to finish any race in life, you must *suffer well*.

As I thought about how best to capture the shared experience of suffering we will all face, my mind was drawn to the idea of a Three Mile Valley. In the Three Mile Valley, the test is actually a lesson that must be learned if we are to live abundantly. Each mile contains a guiding principal of the path that builds into the next mile. When you and I learn the lessons found in the Three Mile Valley, we will suffer well.

The Three Mile Valley is a place of abundant death and abundant life. Every step of the journey is full of redemptive potential, and the path is one of pain and promise. You will learn what I learned, and am still learning, from my tragedy.

You will benefit from the three vital principles found in the Three Mile Valley: think right, do right, and watch God make it all right.

Along the way, you will find key thoughts in shaded rectangles that can unlock greater freedom and strength for your journey. Grab them and take them with you. They will help you through your valley and enrich your life outside of it.

You will also find reflective questions and an action step at the end of each chapter, to help you begin applying these principles to your walk with God through the valleys you face. At the end of each mile, you will find a recap and personal declarations designed to help you suffer well.

Ultimately, of course, the principles contained in this book need to be examined in the light of God's Word, because God holds ultimate authority and possesses the clearest perspective on life.

Are you ready to suffer well? It is time to begin our journey.

CHAPTER ONE

Through the Valley of the Shadow of Death

On November 30, 2011, my family stepped into the darkest valley we have ever encountered. We still walk this valley to this very day. The details of that fateful day are still fresh in my mind, as if it happened yesterday.

The morning started off like any other in my house. None of us had any clue that a storm was raging toward us from just over the horizon. It wasn't an actual weather pattern with clouds, wind, rain, and thunder. It was much, much worse. Everyone was fast asleep, and silence filled the air.

The rudeness of my alarm clock pulled me out of my slumber. With a groan, I forced myself up out of bed to begin my day. After getting ready, I walked out of our bedroom and turned left into my daughter's room. Peyton was already standing in her crib, ready to greet the day.

Her thirteen-month-old gibberish was sounding more and more like English every day. By now she had mastered the most important word in the English language, "Dadda."

Those syllables echoed off the walls of her room and landed straight in my heart that morning. Like every dad, I loved hearing her say my name. Her eyes lit up as I reached down to pick her up.

We enjoyed a simple breakfast as we did most mornings. Peyton loved sharing a banana with me as I took in the peace before my busy day. When it was time for me to head to the office, I transferred parental control to my bride and drove into work.

I was pleasantly interrupted by my cell phone midmorning. It was Marlena with an update on Peyton's doctor visit, a routine check-up for a one-year-old.

A smile stretched across my face as she informed me that the pediatrician said Peyton was perfect. We already knew that.

With our daughter's clean bill of health in hand, Marlena carried on with the rest of her day. What was the plan? A brief lunch stop and then a lengthy nap for our perfect princess.

Perfection was only possible when our little miss didn't miss nap time. She was already beginning to morph into a cranky little lady by the time Marlena got her home and into her crib. Her restoration back to a little bundle of joy would be complete after a short nap.

Peyton was our miracle baby. After our son, Logan, was born, we endured back to back miscarriages. Two heartbreaks in a row were too much to handle. When we found out that Marlena was pregnant for a fourth time, we were cautiously optimistic.

Our cautious optimism transformed into confident optimism as Marlena entered the second trimester. Our confident optimism became complete joy as we welcomed Peyton Elizabeth Herod into the world on October 23, 2010.

Holding her for the first time was surreal. My commitment to Peyton's complete health and wellbeing was iron-clad from the very beginning.

My heart soared that day and every day after Peyton arrived. She was perfect, and the visit to the pediatrician's office had just reminded us of that.

After Marlena finished giving me the update over the phone, she went home to lay Peyton down for a nap. I dove right back into my work at the office.

When I arrived home later that day Peyton was still napping. As I walked into the house Logan greeted me: "Daddy!" Have I mentioned how much I love that word yet? I gave my boy a hug and then grabbed a spot on the floor in front of our living room TV.

Marlena, Logan, and I played some MarioKart on the Wii. We all zipped around the race track as our favorite characters. (Make no mistake, the real competition was between me and Marlena.) At five minutes to five, I squeezed Logan one last time and kissed Marlena good-bye. I got in my car and headed off to speak to students at a youth ministry.

Less than five minutes after leaving, I got the phone call that changed my life forever. It was Marlena. I answered the way I do every time she calls, "Hey Cutie."

She never acknowledged my greeting. What she said next hit me like a tsunami. The panic in her voice let me know that something was terribly wrong. She described every parent's worst nightmare to me in a few short words and ended the phone call by saying, "Come home now!" She hung up to call 911.

My heart raced at a furious pace. I slammed on the brakes of my car and made a U-turn in the middle of the road. My mind spun like a washing machine in its final spin cycle as I replayed Marlena's words over and over. Did I hear her right? How is that possible!?

I sped home and broke several laws along the way. The car screeched to a halt in the driveway. I sprinted into the garage, through the kitchen and down the hall towards Peyton's room.

I turned to enter Peyton's bedroom and was greeted to see my beautiful baby girl laying lifeless on the floor. This was far worse than any nightmare I ever had. It was actually happening. She hadn't been breathing for a while. I fell to my knees, struggling to understand what was happening right in front of my eyes. Marlena administered CPR as I watched in horror. Peyton's chest rose and fell with every breath her loving momma exhaled into her. Seeing this made me feel helpless as a husband and father. I did the only thing I could think to do and laid my hand on Peyton's chest. With all the faith I had, I cried in a whisper, "Jesus, please."

After uttering my two-word prayer, we remembered that our four-year-old son, Logan, was standing just outside Peyton's bedroom in the hallway. I stood to my feet and grabbed him by the hand to go sit on the couch in our living room. As we walked down the hallway the first responders began to arrive.

Our house now filled with intense activity as more first responders arrived. A sheriff, EMTs, and paramedics—a concert of trained professionals all working furiously to bring our little girl back to life.

Our precious princess was placed in the back of the ambulance. It was not looking good at all. The decision was made on the way to the hospital to halt all life-saving attempts. Peyton had passed.

That evening we sat in a hospital room holding our baby girl in our arms, stunned by the reality that she was no longer with us. Shattered and shocked, we struggled to grasp how heaven gained what we had so tragically lost. Our friends and family began to arrive once they heard the news that Peyton was rushed to the hospital. The emergency room waiting area filled now with our loved ones who still did not know the news. Someone needed to tell them.

I walked out of the hospital room and headed toward the waiting room. They had a sense that the news was not good. All I could say in that moment to those within earshot was "She's gone."

We found out later that our beautiful baby girl was taken by Sudden Infant Death Syndrome (SIDS). Ever since that fateful night, we have spent countless hours immersed in grief and covered in tears.

Years have passed since we lost our baby girl, and I am still awash in the intense agony of that tragic night. This chapter has prompted more tears of pain and tears of joy than I can count.

As I write, I wonder what Peyton would look like today. I am confident that she would be beautiful like her momma. And just a little sassy, also like her momma.

Walking through the valley of the shadow of death is extremely difficult. I have grown to see this journey as a walk through the Three Mile Valley. While it will not last forever, we will walk through it for the rest of our lives.

WORKBOOK

Chapter One Questions

Question: "Jesus didn't come to make life easy; He came to make it possible." In what ways do you see our culture expecting Jesus to give an easy life? In what ways have you personally fallen into this way of thinking?

_____

_____

_____

_____

_____

_____

_____

_____

_____

_____

_____

Question: The author describes the personal tragedy that shaped his view of suffering and began his walk through the "Three Mile Valley." Take a moment to journal or share a past or current life event that created ongoing suffering in your life.

_____

_____

_____

_____

_____

_____

_____

_____

_____

_____

Action: Identify someone in your life who is going through a season of suffering (even if you are as well). Commit to praying for this person each day as you read this book. Ask God to reveal other ways that you can reach out and share His comforting presence with them.

Chapter One Notes

_____

_____

_____

_____

_____

_____

_____

_____

_____

_____

_____

_____

_____

_____

_____

_____

_____

_____

_____

_____

_____

CHAPTER TWO

The Three Mile Valley

Losing Peyton has left an indelible scar that my family and I will carry for the rest of our lives. This type of loss is not something that you can "get over." To think that anyone could get over the loss of a loved one is ludicrous. It's also an unhealthy way to grieve and move forward. Marlena and I have committed to carrying the loss of our precious Peyton forward. This book is one way we are choosing to honor her life and remember her as the true gift she was. A true gift she still is.

The challenge that met us the day after our daughter died was larger than us, but not larger than our God. I am happy to say that our marriage is still strong, and our children still look to Jesus as the source of life. We haven't suffered perfectly, and we have quite a bit to learn as we heal. However, we have learned three key principles that we believe will help you suffer well through your own Three Mile Valley.

We want our story to speak louder than our loss and amplify the goodness of God in every circumstance. With God's help, we are walking through the Three Mile Valley and pray that He would help you walk victoriously through yours.

What Is the Three Mile Valley?

The Three Mile Valley is a desolate place full of provision and pain, salvation and suffering, heaven and hell. Abundant life thrives alongside abundant death in this valley.

This place represents your season of suffering. Countless others have valleys that look similar, but no one else has a valley just like yours.

You will never be alone in your valley, but it is yours alone to journey through.

Did God bring you here? Did your choices bring you here? Did the decisions of another person bring you here? The answer to those questions do not matter if you want to get through the Three Mile Valley.

What matters most is how you will walk the path laid out before you. To walk the path, you must understand two truths about the Three Mile Valley. The first truth is that God will never leave you alone in your valley. A well-known psalm says it this way: "Yea, though I walk through the valley of the shadow of death, I will fear no evil; for You are with me; Your rod and Your staff, they comfort me" (Psalms 23:4 NKJV).

God promised that He will be right there with you through every step of the Three Mile Valley. His presence plus your faith response will bring abundant life through the darkest of days.

It was easy for my wife and I ask where God was the night our daughter died. It is a natural question to ask in the middle of any significant pain. This scripture reminds us that God is right here with us, and will be with us as we walk through the entirety of our valley. Sometimes we feel His presence in powerful ways, sometimes we do not. It is reassuring to know that our feelings do not alter the promises of God.

The Shadow of Death

The second truth you must know is that Jesus is greater than the Three Mile Valley. The imagery of the valley of the shadow of death is ominous, wouldn't you agree? You discover that it loses its power after a closer look.

Shadows can only exist because of light. You must remember that there is a greater light when death casts its shadow over your life. That light is Jesus. We know this because He told us in the book of John. You can read it for yourself and discover the powerful promise He gives.

When Jesus spoke again to the people, He said:

> *I am the light of the world. Whoever follows me will never walk in darkness, but will have the light of life.*
> *—John 8:12 (NIV)*

Losing our daughter so suddenly cast a significant shadow over our lives. The deep darkness that still sweeps over our souls on occasion is overwhelming. It is in these moments that I find comfort in the fact that Jesus is the greater light above our tragedy. He is greater than our valley, and He is also greater than yours. While the details of our lives may be different, the Savior who loves us both is the same. He is faithful and true and will never abandon you. Death's ability to cast a shadow is constrained by Jesus' greater existence as the light.

Some stretches of the Three Mile Valley do get dim. Death and other difficulties will cast their shadows over you as you walk. Even so, Jesus has promised that you will never walk in complete darkness. He is the light of life that will guide you every step of the way.

The Three Mile Valley is a place of abundant death. Regardless of how your version of it came to be, it is now your opportunity. Opportunity for what? Death to self. At the core of Jesus' teachings, we find a clear call to die to ourselves.

> Then Jesus told his disciples, "If anyone would come after me, let him deny himself and take up his cross and follow me. For whoever would save his life will lose it, but whoever loses his life for my sake will find it."
> **—Matthew 16:24–25** (ESV)

Difficulties will either make or break you. Suffering is the crucible that expedites growth in our lives when we allow ourselves to be shaped through tough times. When you surrender your life in your pursuit of Jesus—even amid suffering—that is where you will find your life.

This truth about suffering is not popular in our culture. It is much more appealing to embrace a faith that papers over the Biblical concept that suffering is a key part of faith. In writing this book, I hope to peel back that paper and uncover the true and uncomfortable relationship all of us should have with suffering. I am glad that Jesus showed us how to suffer well. Because He did, we can.

Jesus has already walked through this valley for us. He walked through it and conquered it completely. In His darkest moment—when all hope seemed lost and He appeared defeated—the greatest victory was achieved.

This truth changes everything. Because of His power and presence over every valley, I feel it is appropriate to call Him the Master Valley Walker.

He became intimately acquainted with the sufferings of humanity, so that He could be our greatest empathizer when we find ourselves walking through a valley. His example and presence with us teaches us the way. In our journey, we have found Jesus to be the hope in our pain, the light in our darkness, and the peace in our despair. He is everything the Bible reveals Him to be.

As we walk together through the Three Mile Valley, we will learn how to think right, do right, and watch God make it all right. This place can be overwhelming and even scary. There are multiple paths through this valley. Each is unique in its own way.

Chapter Two Questions

Question: When we are going through our own "Three Mile Valley," we are often distracted by questions about who or what is to blame for our pain. What questions are holding you back from facing the deeper issues God is trying to reveal to you? How can you let go of blame and start asking the right questions?

_____

_____

_____

_____

_____

_____

_____

_____

_____

_____

_____

Question: What are some of the sufferings Jesus faced that make Him the Master Valley Walker? List at least five ways He faced suffering while on earth.

_____

_____

_____

_____

_____

_____

_____

_____

_____

Action: Read Isaiah 53:3–4. Compare the sufferings of Jesus with your own. How can you draw comfort from His identification with human suffering?

Chapter Two Notes

_____

_____

_____

_____

_____

_____

_____

_____

_____

_____

_____

_____

_____

_____

_____

_____

_____

_____

_____

_____

CHAPTER THREE

The Four Paths

While all of us will suffer, we will not all suffer the same way. I lost my daughter tragically and suddenly. Your story might be different from mine. You may have lost your health or your job, or you may be battling extreme depression. Just because my loss is different from yours doesn't diminish one or the other. Walking through a season of suffering is hard no matter the exact circumstances.

We are about to begin our journey through the Three Mile Valley, but this valley has four distinct pathways through it. Accordingly, we need to take a look at the four ways we may suffer in this life.

Whichever path you find yourself walking today, however, Jesus has conquered it and will walk you through your specific path to victory.

The Temporary Path

The temporary path is a common path through the Three Mile Valley. There is a very good chance that you have already walked this path at least once in your life. Most people will take multiple journeys through the Three Mile Valley on this path.

This temporary season of suffering can last anywhere from a few weeks to many months. Just because it is a temporary season does not mean it is easy. These temporary seasons can be intense and overwhelming. They can include challenging circumstances like:

- Job loss
- Short-term illnesses
- Unfulfilled expectations
- Discouragement
- Disappointment

Suffering well on the temporary path is very important because of its long-range implications. How you suffer temporarily has the potential to shape how you suffer permanently. Why? The power of precedent is why.

When I was nineteen years old, I was called to serve on jury duty. It was a truly fascinating experience that I will never forget. The court case that I was selected for involved a man who had allegedly used a firearm illegally. Throughout the trial, we heard multiple testimonies and saw a lot of evidence. It was our job, as the jury, to determine whether or not the man on trial was guilty of breaking the law. After much deliberation, we the jury found him guilty, because there was sufficient evidence to convict him. We found out later that this man had a history of breaking the law. What he did before influenced what he did next. In other words, he set a bad precedent in his life by making one bad decision. Instead of changing his behavior, he let the power of precedent prevail and continued to make more bad decisions.

How does this story apply to your temporary path in the Three Mile Valley? I am so glad you asked! You owe it to yourself to suffer well through these temporary seasons of suffering because they will influence your future seasons of suffering. Don't let the name of the path fool you into thinking that it is any less powerful or important. When you suffer well through short-term setbacks, you set yourself up for future victory should you find yourself in the Three Mile Valley again.

The Sustained Path

The duration of the sustained path makes it exceptionally difficult. Every sustained path through the Three Mile Valley has a defined beginning. However, there is no way to know when it will end. Not knowing how long you will walk this path is what makes it so difficult. The challenges that are common on this specific path include:

- Significant relational strife
- Chronic illness
- Financial hardships
- Professional setbacks

When you suffer well on the sustained path, you will avoid the pitfalls of authoring additional hardship for yourself. What do I mean? When there is no end in sight, it is easy to lose sight of what is worth fighting for. You owe it to yourself to steward this season of suffering well, because it is possible to live abundantly while you suffer. When you walk this path wisely, you won't let the unknown timeline of your season undo all the good things that you still have in your life. You will avoid the self-sabotage that is easy to fall into.

The Secret Path

Walking the secret path is difficult because you feel isolated. No one knows you are hurting, or worse yet, you feel like no one cares. Like prison bars on a cell, the solitude of your suffering adds additional layers of pain. You know you are walking the secret path when your circumstance includes:

- Addiction
- Depression
- Unrevealed abuse

A recent survey estimated that 21.5 million Americans meet the criteria for Substance Use Disorder (SUDS).[1] This means that roughly 8 percent of people age twelve and older are addicted to alcohol or illicit drugs. The sobering truth is that this statistic is more than a number to many of you reading this book right now. You have a friend, family member, or coworker who is battling addiction, and it is breaking your heart. I am also keenly aware that you might be the one battling this addiction and are in a fight for your very life.

Your secret path might be addiction, depression, or past emotional trauma that remains unrevealed to this day. You owe it to yourself to suffer well on this path, because freedom is possible. You should be free. Jesus has authored a future for you that is good, and when you steward this season of suffering well, you can be set free.

The Tragic Path

The tragic path is marked by the loss of a loved one. You find yourself on this path when you lose someone whom you never wanted to live without. Like losing an arm, your loss has not ended your own life, but it has undeniably changed it. You now have to learn to live a life you never wanted—a life without your loved one.

The powerful pain in tragic seasons of suffering is found in the presence of your loved one's absence. It is the distinct awareness that they are gone, and all the goodness they authored by their presence is now gone too. Learning to live without someone you love is hard. The soul suffering on this path must learn to live with a new normal. They are forever marked by the tragic loss, and they will carry the scars with them for the rest of their life.

If you are walking the tragic path, first let me say how sorry I am for your loss. You are not alone in your journey, as countless others find themselves on the same path right now.

You owe it to yourself to suffer well on this path for two reasons. 1) You still have your life and it is worth living it abundantly. 2) Suffering well honors the one you lost, because it gives you the opportunity to keep their memory alive as you carry it forward with you.

There are four distinct paths through the Three Mile Valley, and they are all uniquely challenging and powerfully difficult to travel upon. Is it possible that the one path you are walking might merge with another path as you walk through the Three Mile Valley? Absolutely. You should not be surprised if this happens.

You owe it to yourself to suffer well on whatever path through the Three Mile Valley you find yourself. It will not be easy, but because of Jesus it will be possible. He is the Master Valley Walker.

Chapter Three Questions

Question: Would you describe your current suffering as temporary, sustained, secret, or tragic? Which of these paths have you already experienced?

_____

_____

_____

_____

_____

_____

_____

_____

_____

_____

_____

_____

Question: When have you experienced a merging of two paths? How has this interaction of paths affected your journey through the season of suffering?

_____

_____

_____

_____

_____

_____

_____

_____

_____

_____

_____

Action: Journal about your current suffering. Take special note of how God is showing you His grace one day at a time as you walk through the Three Mile Valley.

Chapter Three Notes

CHAPTER FOUR

The Master Valley Walker

Moving forward after any type of loss is difficult. The disappointment and despair that sets in when we suffer is real. It is important to keep living on the other side of loss, even when it is hard. Who you walk with through your valleys is of supreme importance. One of my friends that helped me live after loss is named Steve. He has a knack for getting me to do things that I would never do without him. Call his ideas "stupid" or "outlandish," or whatever you will, but Steve has the uncanny ability to influence my decisions in a good way.

Less than a year after Peyton passed, Steve started talking to me about an adventure race called the Tough Mudder. His master plan included casual dialogue around the idea for a few weeks. Running the Tough Mudder with Steve seemed like a good idea. So good, in fact, that I signed up.

The Tough Mudder is a ten-plus mile race for crazy people. This course ran through stretches of flat prairie, rolled through mud valleys, and crawled up steep hills. Multiple military-style obstacles greeted us along the way.

As we approached the end of our Mudder, we saw Everest. This obstacle stood a full fourteen feet high. The curved wall taunted everyone within view. I watched in awe as several Mudders ascended it with ease. Not everyone was as fortunate. Some slipped, and then slammed into Everest.

My heart raced, and my legs ached. It was my turn. I wondered, "Would the crowd see me standing atop the wall with fists raised high, or sliding like Garfield the Cat on a bad day?" I give you full permission to laugh at what happened next.

I ran with everything I had up the curved wall. I reached—and I missed the top edge. I slid back down the wall. Everest proved to be too high a mountain for me to climb.

I was down, but not out. I ran back to the starting point, ready for another shot. While I wasn't looking, a friend of mine conquered the curved wall. He then turned around to help whoever was next. That person was me.

Everest beckoned me again. Running as fast as I could, I ascended the curved wall and reached for my friend's hand. We connected. He helped me overcome the wall. We climbed down off that mountain together.

The greatness of the moment was not lost on me. Who I kept close to in that moment dramatically impacted the outcome. Because I was near someone who conquered the obstacle in front of me, I conquered it too.

Jesus Is the Master Valley Walker

What do you do when you are eyeball-deep in a circumstantial sea of suffering? Who will you turn to when your situation is an unscalable uphill climb? Where will you find strength when life feels more like a three-mile valley than a mountain top?

You need someone who knows the terrain better than you do. You need the Master Valley Walker. Regardless of the specific path you may walk, you can know that someone greater has already gone before you. This truth is found in the following verse from the Gospel of John.

In John 16:33 (NLT) Jesus declares:

> *I have told you all this so that you may have peace in me. Here on earth you will have many trials and sorrows. But take heart, because I have overcome the world.*

When I hear bad news or a negative report, I want it to come layered in optimism. I love the way that Jesus tells it like it is. He pulls no punches as He tells us how life is going to go.

Let's look at the first layer of John 16:33.

Jesus promises us peace in Him. For the one who is suffering, peace is power because it can calm the storm inside of you. His presence in your valley is a game changer. When you follow Jesus, peace is not the absence of opposition—it is the presence of someone greater.

His presence promises peace as your problems promise pain. Your pain may be powerful, but Jesus is so much greater.

Peace is not the absence of opposition.
It is the presence of someone greater.

Jesus gave us the good news, and now it is time for some bad news. According to Him, we will have "many trials and sorrows." Multiple. More than one. It should come as no surprise that some stretches of life will break us down.

Suffering in life is not a probability—it is a promise.

Now for more good news. Jesus has conquered every sickness, setback, dysfunction, and disease that you will ever encounter. He didn't just battle on our behalf, He overcame in our place. This makes him the Master Valley Walker. Jesus has already conquered your darkest day and your loneliest night. You no longer have to suffer in solitude because your valley has the footprints of Jesus all over it. He suffered in your place to bring you peace in every place you suffer.

What does this all mean for you? Much like my friend stood atop the curved wall to help me in the Tough Mudder, Jesus now stands on top of the Three Mile Valley with

His hand stretched out to help you. To receive His help, you simply need to reach up and grab his hand. In an instant, abundant life is infused into your soul and victory in the valley becomes possible.

Jesus invites all of us into a life of victory. He wants to help us through the Three Mile Valley and release abundant life in us and through us. He gives us strength to overcome our seasons of suffering and the power to walk in victory every day. Who you walk with through your valley changes everything. Jesus is someone you want to follow on your journey.

Chapter Four Questions

Question: Sometimes we try to find strength apart from the Lord. What are some common places that people look for comfort and peace when they are in a valley? Where do you seek strength and peace in difficulty?

_____

_____

_____

_____

_____

_____

_____

_____

_____

_____

_____

Question: How do you respond to the inevitability of suffering? Does that reality fill you with fear, anger, or frenzy? How can you look to the future with hope and peace?

_____

_____

_____

_____

_____

_____

_____

_____

_____

_____

_____

Action: What are some tangible reminders that help you realize God's presence in your pain? Music, art, scriptures, and creation can all speak to us of God's nature as we walk through our darkest valley. Choose one of these reminders that has meant a lot to you and share it with the suffering friend for whom you are praying.

Chapter Four Notes

_____

_____

_____

_____

_____

_____

_____

_____

_____

_____

_____

_____

_____

_____

_____

_____

_____

_____

_____

_____

INTO THE VALLEY

Now Entering the Three Mile Valley

It's time to begin our journey through the Three Mile Valley. What does it look like?

Picture a valley that stretches three miles long. Each mile contains unique terrain that amplifies a principle of the path. Mile one is a flat and barren expanse that appears lifeless on every level. It looks like it goes on forever. Right thinking is the key to conquering this mile.

Mile two is a craggy and uneven stretch of the valley. Each step you take is critical, because choosing right is the key to conquering this mile.

Mile three welcomes you with hopeful signs of life and renewal. Watching God make everything all right is the key to conquering this mile.

A set of verses from the book of James has guided my family through our journey through the Three Mile Valley:

> *Consider it pure joy, my brothers and sisters, whenever you face trials of many kinds, because you know that the testing of your faith produces perseverance. Let perseverance finish its work so that you may be mature and complete, not lacking anything.*
>
> *—James 1:2–4 (NIV)*

These three verses serve as the foundation for the three principles of the path you are about to discover waiting in every mile: think right, do right, and watch God make it all right. Let's explore these principles as we journey through the Three Mile Valley together.

CHAPTER FIVE

The First Mile:
Now Is Not Forever

The first mile of the Three Mile Valley is distinctively flat. It looks like it goes on forever. Barren and lifeless on every level, this mile is full of discouragement. The first mile can only be conquered one way. You must learn to think right.

I had no idea how difficult the Three Mile Valley could be. The weeks and months that followed Peyton's passing were the darkest moments of my life. Simple office work became difficult. Normal conversation proved near impossible. When I let my mind wander, her absence would overwhelm me.

My "now" felt like it would be my "forever." I wondered more than once: *Will I ever get through this?*

Like seeing a mirage in a desert, the Three Mile Valley will make you feel what is not real. You will feel like your pain will never end. You will feel like the darkness will never leave. You will feel all this and more.

It is temporary. All of it. You need to know this truth now more than ever before. The principle of the path that we learn in the first mile is this: *now is not forever.* This truth empowers us to suffer well through the Three Mile Valley.

Now Is Not Forever—Think Right

Your three-mile trial will not last forever. God has imposed limits on every season. Take a look at the words of Ecclesiastes chapter 3.

For everything there is a season, a time for every activity under heaven.

A time to be born and a time to die.

A time to plant and a time to harvest.

A time to kill and a time to heal.

A time to tear down and a time to build up.

A time to cry and a time to laugh.

A time to grieve and a time to dance.

A time to scatter stones and a time to gather stones.

A time to embrace and a time to turn away.

A time to search and a time to quit searching.

A time to keep and a time to throw away.

A time to tear and a time to mend.

A time to be quiet and a time to speak.

A time to love and a time to hate. A time for war and a time for peace.

—Ecclesiastes 3:1–8 (NLT)

Verse 4 is especially beautiful: "A time to cry and a time to laugh. A time to grieve and a time to dance." God reminds us that although we cry, we will not cry forever. The sounds of our sorrow will be replaced by joyful laughter. Our grief will be replaced with dancing. The pit of despair will be filled with vibrant celebration. Someday. Every season of suffering has an expiration date. Keep this in focus as you move forward through the Three Mile Valley.

Your perspective will either produce or prevent perseverance in your valley.

Your victory in this valley begins in your mind—it is imperative that you think right about your circumstances. When you think rightly about your season, you have perspective. When you have perspective, you find strength to persevere. And when you persevere, your journey moves in the right direction.

It is time for you to go Pro in your thought life. This will require commitment and will not be easy. To go Pro, you must choose a productive perspective. A *productive* perspective *pro*duces perseverance in your life. Thinking the right way elevates you to the major league of abundant life to which Jesus calls all of us.

When you go Pro in your thought life, you go on the offensive. Read the following verse and focus on the second half.

> *We demolish arguments and every pretension that sets itself up against the knowledge of God, and we take captive every thought to make it obedient to Christ.*
> **—2 Corinthians 10:5** (NIV)

The thoughts you let roam free in your mind shape your perspective. Any thoughts that are in line with the gospel are *pro*ductive and lead to perseverance. Every thought must be strained through this filter of truth. This is how you elevate your thought life and rise up to suffer well.

To go Pro in your thought life, you shun unproductive perspectives. This is key because an unproductive perspective prevents perseverance. You want to avoid this pitfall that befalls so many in the Three Mile Valley. Take every thought captive and bring it into alignment with Jesus. You can walk in victory because Jesus is your victory. Now is not forever.

Perspective is difficult to find sometimes—especially when you are in pain. There will be times in every valley that will discourage you. When you are discouraged, you will be tempted to quit. It is at this point that you should employ the fighter's countdown.

The Fighter's Countdown

The fighter's countdown is a series of questions you ask yourself when you struggle to find perspective in your valley.

- Can I make it another month?
  - o Yes: Keep going, you're gonna make it.
  - o No: Ask the next question.

- Can I make it another week?
  - o Yes: Keep going, you're gonna make it.
  - o No: Ask the next question.

- Can I make it through today?
  - o Yes: Keep going, you're gonna make it.
  - o No: Ask the next question.

- Can I make it through the next hour?
    - Yes: Keep going, you're gonna make it.
    - No: Ask the next question.

- Can I make it through the next minute?
    - Yes: Keep going, you're gonna make it.
    - No: Just breathe. You're gonna make it.

It is okay to admit when your season of suffering proves too much for you. You're not supposed to have it all figured out. That is God's job. Your job in your valley is to suffer well. When you know that now is not forever, you can keep yourself together even when your world is falling apart.

When our daughter died, a part of me died too. The pain of losing Peyton still threatens to paralyze me today. Because I know that now is not forever, I believe that God will resurrect the part of me that died on that fateful night. Someday.

Until then, I will suffer well, as I remember that this valley is not my home. As I walk through this valley of the shadow of death, I know that my stay here is temporary. Your journey through your valley is temporary too. Keep this in perspective to think rightly through your suffering and persevere through it. You and I are passing through the Three Mile Valley.

What you see is not what you get.
What you see is what you must get through.

God's way of thinking is the right way of thinking. Learning to think differently is quite challenging in the natural. Learning to think God's way is supernatural. Consider just how important the transformation of your thought processes is to God in the following verse:

> *Do not conform to the pattern of this world, but be transformed by the renewing of your mind. Then you will be able to test and approve what God's will is—his good, pleasing and perfect will.*
> **—Romans 12:2** *(NIV)*

We aren't supposed to suffer like the rest of the world suffers. The pattern of the world when it comes to suffering is to lose perspective and miss how God sees this moment.

When your mind is renewed, so is your vision. God wants you to think the best thoughts because He knows what happens when you do. Allow God to help you think right through your valley. It is a cooperative effort that requires you to spend time in God's Word.

If you want to know what God is thinking, read the Bible. This simple discipline will renew your mind and further the good work that God is accomplishing in your life.

Marlena and I both regularly look to Scripture as we navigate the loss of our daughter. We know enough to know that God knows what He is talking about, and that we had better be paying attention to Him in the places of our pain. The Bible is replete with teachings and examples of God's perspective on life. It is wise for you and me to read it all for ourselves.

Our journey through the Three Mile Valley has just begun. I believe that your victory in your valley has begun too. You can keep yourself together when you know that now is not forever.

Conquering the first mile of the Three Mile Valley requires you and I to think right. There is something else you need to know as we walk through this first mile: It is okay to ask questions.

Chapter Five Questions

Question: How would you describe the season you are in right now? What are some tangible ways you can remind yourself that it is not forever?

_____

_____

_____

_____

_____

_____

_____

_____

_____

_____

_____

Question: What thought patterns make you want to give up or leave you overwhelmed with doubts? How can you replace these with right—biblical—thinking?

_____

_____

_____

_____

_____

_____

_____

_____

_____

_____

_____

Action: The Bible lets us know what God is thinking. If you are not already in God's Word on a daily basis, commit that for the next month you will read a portion of Scripture each day. If you aren't sure where to start, the Psalms and the Gospels (Matthew, Mark, Luke, and John) are great sources of comfort through a season of suffering.

Chapter Five Notes

CHAPTER SIX

The First Mile:
"Why?" Is a Good Question

Several years before Peyton passed, I stood staring at a reflection that I did not recognize. I knew something was terribly wrong.

The morning my reflection changed was like every other morning. It was a Friday, which happened to be my day off. It began well and kept getting better. I had no idea that by sunset that evening, I would be staring a horrific reality in the face.

The sun was shining, and there was snow on the ground. My son, Logan, was ready to play outside. At three years old, he was a spot of sunshine in our house. His contagious laughter could light up a room. After some breakfast, we bundled up and headed outside.

We had a great time as we rolled around in the snow and blasted each other with snowballs. When the shenanigans subsided, it was time to head inside and warm back up. This great morning transitioned into an awesome afternoon, which later became a fun night out with friends.

When the babysitter arrived later that evening, Marlena and I loaded up and headed out to see a movie. I had no idea that I was hours away from a permanent life change.

As I sat in the movie theater, I noticed my left eye begin to burn a little bit. It wasn't bad, just annoying. The pain intensified as I watched the movie on the big screen. Then tears began to flow out of the same eye that burned. I knew at that point that something was wrong.

When the ending credits rolled, I made a beeline to the bathroom. I found a mirror and discovered that my face didn't look right. I took in a deep breath and told myself that I was okay.

Our group of friends went out to eat after the movie. More tears flowed down the one side of my face. More pain seared through my left eye. Then, when I took a drink of my soda, I was shocked by what happened. My lips could not form a seal around the straw! The carbonated liquid fizzed as it dribbled down my chin and onto my shirt. I scrambled for a napkin and quickly cleaned up the spill. My friends told me later that they were worried at that point. It was clear to them that I was not okay.

I had never experienced anything like that before. My mind raced as I wondered, *What in the world is happening to me?!*

We arrived home at the end of the evening. I needed to find a mirror fast. Horror gripped my heart as I stood in front of my bathroom mirror. I was face-to-face with a reflection I did not recognize. The person looking back at me was *disfigured*. The left side of the man's face was paralyzed. Was this really happening to *me*?

When I raised my eyebrows, only one of them went up! When I smiled, my mouth pulled to the right side of my face. When I blinked, my left eye stayed open. I quickly called to my wife and said, "Look at me!" Her response? "It's not that bad." I could not have disagreed more.

That night I went to bed with tape over my left eye to keep it shut. I prayed I would wake up and be okay. Maybe it was all just a bad dream. My wish was not granted.

Bell's palsy. That is what happened to the left side of my face. It strikes with little to no warning and presents in varying degrees of severity. It includes a paralysis that often affects one side of the face and causes some drooping, often noticeable. My doctor prescribed medication and told me that I would better in two weeks. I immediately started taking the prescribed medicine—I wanted to get better fast!

Three months later, I still showed no signs of improvement. I wondered if I would have this facial paralysis for the rest of my life.

Have you ever looked in the mirror and been unimpressed by what you see? Have you ever struggled to focus in a conversation because all you can think about is everything that is wrong with you? This was my world for five straight months.

My Bell's palsy brought me face to face with intense physical—and emotional—pain. It forced me to ask the question that we all ask when we suffer: *Why does God*

allow pain? This question has been at the heart of countless theological debates throughout the centuries, but
when I faced it head-on, it drove me to despair.

Even though the answer to this question will not
change our circumstances, we still ask it. *Why, God?
Why?*

It's a good question to ask, but it can be unproductive.

The Well of "Why?"

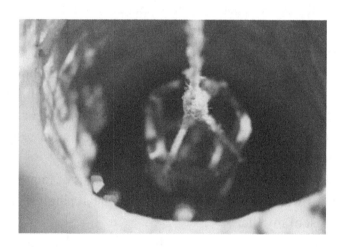

As we journey through the first mile of the Three Mile
Valley, we find a place that represents our honest response
to hard times. It is an old-style, stone-walled well with a
bucket resting on the rim. It is just off the beaten path and
easy enough to get to, so we walk over to it.

Upon our arrival, we see a sign affixed to the top of the
well. It reads: *The Well of "Why?"*

We look at each other and shrug. What could it hurt? We take turns lowering the bucket deep into the dark cavern below. Time after time, the bucket hits the bottom of the well with a loud splash. The bucket disappears under the water as it fills up. However, as the bucket ascends the circular shaft of the well, we discover it to be cracked, full of holes, and leaking fast. By the time the bucket gets up to us, it is empty. We try another time to see if working harder to get the bucket up to the top faster will at least let us get a small taste of water. Alas, the bucket comes up empty again.

In a sense of sheer irony, the exercise that is intended to quench our thirst, has only amplified it. This is the paradox that is the Well of "Why?" After some time, it becomes clear to you and me that interacting with the Well of "Why?" intensifies our thirst rather than satisfying it. In other words, asking "Why?" is often better at creating more questions than it is at providing answers.

Lingering at this well regularly disappoints. We ask why when pain prevents progress. We ask why when our circumstantial dissonance is hard to handle.

It is natural and normal to ask why. We aren't wrong when we ask it. However, we should not pin our hopes of healing on any answer we receive. Some answers will make our journey through the Three Mile Valley even harder.

What you really want when you ask why?—Is an answer. But what you really need is strength for the next step. God spoke to this suffering question long before we could ask it.

"My thoughts are nothing like your thoughts," says the LORD. "And my ways are far beyond anything you could imagine. For just as the heavens are higher than the earth, so my ways are higher than your ways and my thoughts higher than your thoughts."

—Isaiah 55:8–9 (NLT)

God sees things differently than we do. His perspective is unconstrained by time and space. He has no limits on how far back He can see. And looking forward, He is able to comprehend every future possibility.

I don't know about you, but I think that's impressive.

Let's imagine that God fully explained why He allows you to suffer. In His explanation, He live-streams a full multimedia presentation down to your smartphone. It is complete with graphs and flowcharts. He breaks it all down in plain language, and He gives you all the time that you need to think it through. As a bonus, He opens up a conversation to address your follow-up questions.

Do you think you would be content with the answers? Is that what you really wanted?

More times than I can count, I have wondered why God allowed my daughter to die. If God were to explain His reasoning, complete with a multimedia presentation and feedback options, I am confident that I would still disagree with His explanations.

More than an answer, I want my pain to stop. My finite mind assumes that the limitless God could easily author another outcome for us. Additionally, if I believe that God is the one who causes all my pain, then I am left to reconcile what that means.

The Lord's Prayer begins with the well-known phrase, "Our Father in heaven, hallowed be your name" (Matthew 6:9, NIV). The specific verse records Jesus teaching us how to pray. He intentionally begins by identifying God as a heavenly father. Yes, God is the creator, our judge, deliverer, redeemer, and more. The fact that Jesus teaches us to see God as our heavenly father is key. He will discipline us (Hebrews 12:7) and refine us (John 15:1–2) because He is a good father.

Does this mean that every single thing happens to us because God makes it happen?

In response to our loss, several people told us, "Everything happens for a reason." I have struggled to understand what that means. I don't believe for one moment that everything happens for a reason. If everything happens for a reason, then I have to ask: For whose reason does it happen?

The implication with that statement is that *God* causes everything to happen for a reason. That His hand causes rapists to rape, murderers to murder, and liars to lie—all because "He has a purpose." But that isn't the case.

This belief does not account for the gift of free will that God has placed inside each one of us. This belief is crippling because it lays the blame for every atrocity, loss, and heartache squarely at the feet of God.

It is hard to pray to a god that causes you nothing but pain. But thankfully, there is a better way to view suffering.

God does not make everything happen for a reason;
He gives a purpose to everything that happens.

God alone is powerful enough to take the exponential potential of the human experience and make sense of it all. He does not *make* everything happen for a reason; He *gives* everything that happens a reason. This belief empowers us to pray to the One who is not the source of all our pain, but who is the hope for all our healing.

When we choose to believe that God gives a purpose to everything that happens, we set ourselves up to get the why along the way. Because now is not forever, there is still time for God to work out our circumstances for our good. I want you to take a look at a verse from Romans that has given me great hope for my journey through the Three Mile Valley.

> *And we know that for those who love God all things work together for good, for those who are called according to his purpose.*
> **—Romans 8:28** *(ESV)*

This promise is powerful, and it is for you. When you love God, your pain takes on a greater purpose. Our Heavenly Father goes to work in every situation to forge a future that is good for us from His eternal perspective. When we ask why and refuse to move until we get an answer, we limit the life that we can live. But when we ask why as we move forward, we set ourselves up for the purpose that God will give our pain if we keep walking with Him.

Should we stop trying to figure out the purpose behind our pain? No. There is a significance in suffering that brings a perspective that is unattainable apart from it.

We must remember that God doesn't expect us to understand it all. He never has and He never will. However, He does call us to trust Him with childlike faith as we walk through the Three Mile Valley.

It is time to continue our journey. We know that there is purpose in our pain. We must choose to walk forward through this valley and trust that God will help us understand someday. We don't need to know all of the answers to life's most difficult questions when we know the One who does.

WORKBOOK

Chapter Six Questions

Question: Have you ever been stuck at the Well of "Why?" Did it ultimately help or hinder your healing? Why is it so difficult to accept that we will never know *why* some things happen?

_____

_____

_____

_____

_____

_____

_____

_____

_____

_____

_____

Question: "God does not make everything happen for a reason; He gives a purpose to everything that happens." How is this statement consistent with both God's sovereignty and man's free will? Why is it important to see God as the Redeemer instead of the Author of our pain?

_____

_____

_____

_____

_____

_____

_____

_____

_____

_____

_____

Action: It's time to leave the Well of "Why?" behind! As you continue your journey, focus on the purpose with which God infuses your pain. Look for specific ways to use your pain productively—to help others in their suffering.

Chapter Six Notes

CHAPTER SEVEN

The First Mile:
"How?" Is the Best Question

Wrestling with questions is a healthy part of the journey through the Three Mile Valley. But there is one question that, when answered, will help you find the road map to victory. That question is: *How can I suffer well?* This pivot away from every other question is where spirituality and practicality collide. Our response to this question is very important, because faith flows from an active response to God's Word.

When you reach up to grab Jesus' hand, you embark on a unique journey, full of both the miraculous and the mundane. Simultaneously awe-inspiring and awful, it is paradoxical at its core. Read the words of Jesus here as He outlines the terms of His offer:

> Then Jesus said to his disciples, "Whoever wants to be my disciple must deny themselves and take up their cross and follow me. For whoever wants to save their life will lose it,

but whoever loses their life for me will find it. What good will it be for someone to gain the whole world, yet forfeit their soul? Or what can anyone give in exchange for their soul? For the Son of Man is going to come in his Father's glory with his angels, and then he will reward each person according to what they have done."
      —Matthew 16:24–27 (NIV)

You and I are called to deny ourselves and carry our cross in every season of life. Just because we are suffering does not mean that we should put our cross down. Suffering well is the call of the cross in every circumstance we will ever face. The Three Mile Valley is, quite vividly, our opportunity to identify with the suffering of our Savior and to become more like Him.

As we carry our cross forward, the old sinful "self" inside each of us decreases and Christ increases. In other words, abundant death to self-centered living makes ample room for Jesus to resurrect abundant life in us and release it through us. The inspired writer of Philippians captures the essence of our pilgrimage this way:

I want to know Christ—yes, to know the power of his resurrection and participation in his sufferings, becoming like him in his death, and so, somehow, attaining to the resurrection from the dead.
      —Philippians 3:10–11 (NIV)

Suffering is not a probability; it is a promise with a purpose. And that purpose, regardless of the details specific to each of our lives, is ultimately to bring us closer to Jesus. Let this truth sink in! Our pain makes us the pupil in the classroom of life. And here is the lesson we all must learn: In the Three Mile Valley, *we gain* through loss, setback, and disappointment. Pain's power is restrained by the hand of God as He guides us closer to Himself.

One of the fastest ways to get to know someone else is to suffer with them. This simple yet challenging exercise provides insight and perspective to another person that you might not gain any other way. In the same way, hardship is a fast track to a closer walk with Jesus. You discover Him in despair, and you meet Him in the mess as He holds you through your moments of hell on earth. He may not have authored your pain, but He will author good things *through* your pain.

> *Suffering is not a probability;*
> *it is a promise with a purpose.*

Thinking right is the key to conquering the Three Mile Valley. When your thoughts are saturated by the truth, you have what you need to proceed in victory. This in no way implies that suffering will be *easier* when you think right. Suffering is hard by definition. When you suffer well you will still shed tears, cry out in frustration, and come face to face with the real and raw you. But thinking right through the Three Mile Valley empowers you to hold fast to the promises found in God's Word. It focuses your mind on the One who has already conquered the world. He is greater than your deepest valley, and He now walks alongside of you.

Your perspective will either precede or prevent perseverance in your life. When your mind is aligned with the truth, you can overcome anything and everything that stands in your way. You owe it to yourself to think right through the Three Mile Valley. Embracing the fact that suffering is a part of the faith that saves you, empowers you to ask the best question in the face of suffering: How? Focusing on how you will suffer is practical and productive. Like guardrails on a road, this question will drive you forward and keep you from veering off into other places that won't help you get to where you ultimately need to be. In my experience, I have sometimes found that my response in the Three Mile Valley is the only thing I can control.

You need to shift your focus from asking why God would allow pain, to asking the best question instead: *How can I suffer well?* When you ask this question, you position yourself to gain more than you could ever lose. Your thoughts will flow in the most productive direction possible: forward.

WORKBOOK

Chapter Seven Questions

Question: How do you feel about the concept of suffering well? Do you think it is possible to suffer well even in extremely difficult circumstances? Why or why not?

_____

_____

_____

_____

_____

_____

_____

_____

_____

_____

_____

Question: "Suffering is not a probability; it is a promise with a purpose." How does this statement affect your attitude toward suffering?

_____

_____

_____

_____

_____

_____

_____

_____

_____

_____

_____

Action: Develop a personal mission statement of how you plan to suffer well. Make your statement succinct and easy to remember, as well as something that can bring you back to a right perspective on difficult days.

Chapter Seven Notes

CHAPTER EIGHT

The First Mile: Remember Who You Are

When I was in elementary school, I made a mistake that I have carried ever since. It happened one day when I had too much free time. My boredom led me to explore our family bathroom. I rummaged through drawers and even the medicine cabinet.

My eyes shot wide open when I found my dad's razor. It was an old-school, two-sided model. The top opened to reveal the razor blade inside. My little fingers reached for the blade and pulled it out.

I marveled at the edges of the rectangular metal. It easily flipped end over end in my hand. That stopped being fun real fast. I neatly placed it back where it came from. That is when I saw the extra pack of razor blades in the drawer.

My comfort level with the shiny blades was illogically high. I removed one sharp rectangle from the pack. My curiosity would not let me put it down—that is, until I got bored. I slid the razor back into the box and suddenly felt the searing pain of the blade cutting my middle finger. I bled quite profusely as I screamed for help.

My dad, who is quite deaf, came running into the bathroom. Apparently, I had screamed so loudly that even he heard it. He applied appropriate pressure to my wound and stopped the bleeding. I did not need stitches for my finger, but I could have used some for my ego. I felt stupid for making a mistake like that.

In time, my finger healed, and a scar appeared. I can still see it today. My scar is something I have on my body to remind me of what happened, but it is not who I am. While I may have bruised my ego by making a bad decision, the proof of a past mistake does not define who I am today. I have the scar. It does not have me.

You are more than the sum of your scars.
You are held by the One who holds the stars.

Walking through the Three Mile Valley is difficult. You will accumulate your share of scars as you journey forward. Each one is a permanent reminder of a bad experience, but the pain will pass. Remember, you are not your scars. You belong to the One with nail scarred hands.

Your tragedy is not your identity.

The world tells us that the defining power of pain in our lives cements who we are. Because of Jesus, however, we can differentiate who we are from what we go through. We must not confuse our identity with our experiences.

After Peyton passed, I discovered that my valley wanted to take more than my daughter from me. It reached for the very essence of who I was and still am. Over time I lost sight of the truth about my identity. I forgot who God said that I was.

This created an ugly pride inside of me. I allowed my identity to shift away from the foundation of God's Word and onto the shifting sands of circumstance. Pride grew inside me because I thought that I was a survivor. This affected everything. I looked at myself differently. I looked at others differently.

I was wrong. I am not a survivor. Here is why. A survivor's identity is rooted in the past. It is connected to something they can never change. This identity permeates everything. Like a badge proudly worn—it is on full display for everyone to see.

Jesus didn't come to make me a survivor. He came to make me a conqueror. The difference is dynamic. Jesus doesn't ask us to live through hard times; He calls us to overcome them.

No, in all these things we are more than conquerors through him who loved us.
—Romans 8:37 *(NIV)*

Remember who you are as you walk through the Three Mile Valley. Hear the declaration of scripture that boldly declares who you really are—more than a conqueror.

A survivor you are not! You are more than a conqueror in Christ. His victory has changed your identity in every circumstance. You are now an unstoppable overcomer in Christ. Living in victory is more than what you do; it is the overflow of who you are through Him who loves you.

Your identity is not circumstantial; it is providential.

You may feel like your situation is a complete loss. Because you are a conqueror, however, you need to fight until the end. As long as there is time, you have a choice to make. Believe the truth about yourself and know that you will overcome your darkest day, even when it feels like it is fading into a darker night.

On the cross, Jesus was crowned the Victor. Through the cross, that crown benefits us. Please don't miss this! Center who you are on Christ. When you do, you will know beyond a shadow of a doubt that your identity is not up for debate. I love the way the Holy Spirit gets into the valley with us and reminds us of who we are. Read the following verses from Romans and see for yourself.

The Spirit himself bears witness with our spirit that we are children of God, and if children, then heirs—heirs of God and fellow heirs with Christ, provided we suffer with him in order that we may also be glorified with him.
—Romans 8:16–17 (ESV)

We are identified as the children of God in our suffering. The inheritance we now qualify for is eternal. We are merely passing through as we make our way to the full and abundant life that Jesus purchased for us.

What if your valley is a result of your own doing, like the scar of a little boy who was playing with his daddy's razor blade?

I know what some of you are thinking. You believe that your actions are too much for God to redeem. That your mess is too messy for God to still love you.

I have good news for you. Setbacks, mistakes, and heartaches authored by your own hand lose their suffocating power when you know who you are. God's grace is sufficient for you, even when you make mistakes. Your identity in Christ is stronger than any string of bad decisions.

You are not the sum of your mistakes. You are not your scars. You are not destined to fail; you have been called to win, so press on until the end.

The Three Mile Valley will undeniably shape you, but it does not have to define you. Think right thoughts and remember that who you are has nothing to do with where you are or what you are going through.

Now is not forever. You are more than a conqueror in Christ.

WORKBOOK

Chapter Eight Questions

Question: What scar(s) from the past have you allowed to define you? How does that definition of your identity differ from Christ's identity for you?

_____

_____

_____

_____

_____

_____

_____

_____

_____

_____

_____

Question: How does taking on the identity of "more than a conqueror" change your perspective on your circumstances?

_____

_____

_____

_____

_____

_____

_____

_____

_____

_____

_____

Action: Make a list of the identity traits that you have received in Christ, as found in Scripture (e.g., "I am accepted in the Beloved," "I am a new creation," "I am more than a conqueror"). Write or print out the list and put it in a place where you will see it often.

Chapter Eight Notes

_____

_____

_____

_____

_____

_____

_____

_____

_____

_____

_____

_____

_____

_____

_____

_____

_____

_____

_____

_____

_____

_____

FIRST MILE RECAP

Remember,
Now Is Not Forever

Thinking right is the key to conquering the first mile of the Three Mile Valley. The truth is that you and I are pilgrims on a path that leads through this moment. We will not stay in this place of pain and suffering forever. What we see is not what will forever be. It is okay to ask questions. The natural response to heartache and loss is to be perplexed and wonder what happened. We must remember that God is not afraid of our questions, but we might not understand His answers. He thinks differently about our journey because His thoughts and His ways are higher than ours.

Keeping that in mind, then pivot to the most productive question in your suffering and ask yourself how you will suffer well. You will find the beginning to this answer when you align your mind with the truth. This means that you will remember who you are in Christ. You are not the sum of your mistakes or the totality of your offenses. Your loss is unable to subtract the essence of your identity as a conqueror. No longer a victim, you now stand as the victor because of Jesus. When you think right in the Three Mile Valley, you begin to suffer well.

Declarations to Help You Align Your Mind:

- Jesus didn't come to make my life easy. He came to make my life abundant.
- God's presence in the valley, plus my faith response, unleashes abundant life in me and through me.
- Peace is not the absence of opposition. It is the presence of someOne greater.
- Suffering in life is not a probability. It is a promise with a purpose.
- Following Jesus takes priority over my comfort.
- I am going pro in my thought life. My *pro*ductive perspective will *pro*duce perseverance.
- What I see is not what I get. What I see is what I must get through.
- My tragedy is not my identity.
- I am more than the sum of my scars; I am held by the One who holds the stars.
- My identity is not circumstantial; it is providential.
- God gives everything that happens a reason. He has the last word in my story.

CHAPTER NINE

The Second Mile:
Cherish Your Choice

Congratulations! You have made it through the first mile. You have learned that now is not forever. Take this right thinking forward with you into the second mile, as we explore how to suffer well. The second mile is a craggy and uneven stretch of the valley. Each step you take is critical, because choosing right is the key to conquering this mile.

A while back, I was returning from El Salvador at the end of a short-term mission trip. Seated across the aisle from me on my flight was a nice woman from El Salvador. I speak some Spanish, and I confess that I had eavesdropped, picking up the light conversation that she had had with her husband and daughter earlier in the flight.

When the pilot began his transition from flying to landing, the woman seated next to me also began her own transition. She stopped being really nice and started being really nervous. For the rest of the flight, we will appropriately refer to her as *Nancy Nerviosa* (Nervous Nancy).

Suddenly, the cabin lights went dark. Our anxious friend climbed to a fresh level of concern. Dimming the cabin lights is standard protocol for landing on some flights, but it was an unwelcome change for *Nancy Nerviosa*. I heard her whisper under her breath, *"Dios mio!"* ("Oh my God!"). She grabbed the armrests with a kung-fu death-grip level of ferocity.

Then vapor clouds began to pour out of the ceiling ventilation system. This is normal and occasionally happens because of the atmospheric changes that accompany the descent. I thought it looked pretty cool in the dimly lit atmosphere. Not so for *Nancy Nerviosa*.

We hit turbulence, and she screamed *"Ay!"* as she braced herself. She was terrified! We descended further and further, until the back wheels of the plane touched the runway—and then the front wheels. *Nancy Nerviosa* couldn't take much more. It is a good thing we were almost there. She employed her invisible plane brake pedal on the floor in front of her. Man, did she stomp on that imaginary braking system! Any harder, and she might have kicked someone in first class!

The plane drew down to a safe and slow taxiing speed, and she let out a *"Gracias a Dios!"* ("Thank You, God!").

I said *yes* and *amen* to that.

What if *Nancy Nerviosa* had been unable to keep herself together? Who would have helped her? The flight attendants would have. They oversaw the flight, because they were stewarding it. Fully committed to responding to whatever might happen, these women and men help us understand what it means to make the best out of every situation.

In the second mile of our journey, we discover that it isn't enough to think right thoughts. We must take right actions if we are to suffer well.

Cherish Your Choice by Doing Right

You and I are stewards in our season of suffering. We suffer well when we understand that we are responsible for our response to painful experiences. While many seasons of suffering begin through no fault of our own, we still must steward the season if we want to suffer well. As followers of Jesus, we are called to live wisely. Take a look at these verses from Ephesians that shape how we should see our journey through the Three Mile Valley.

> *Be very careful, then, how you live—not as unwise but as wise, making the most of every opportunity, because the days are evil.*
> **—Ephesians 5:15–16** *(NIV)*

Your valley is full of opportunities. While it may not feel like it, every step forward is another opportunity to make the most out of your valley. You owe it to yourself to make wise choices when life is hard. You owe it to your loved ones to steward your pain with wisdom. You owe it to God to humbly endeavor to make every choice throughout your Three Mile Valley a wise one.

Your response is your responsibility.

No one else can steward your valley for you. No one else is responsible for the way you go through your valley. You may not be able to control your circumstances, but you can influence how you live through it.

When you suffer well, you live knowing that you have a significant part to play in your story. You commit to carrying what you alone can carry. Your response to hardship is your responsibility.

This truth is both liberating and sobering.

It is liberating, because you know that you do have a choice in the matter. Even though circumstances may instigate a sense of chaos, God has given you a powerful gift during the storm: your response. What you do is up to you.

It is also sobering, because you can sense the weight of ownership that your choices create. God's grace will be enough for you on your darkest day. Should your response be unwise, God will faithfully walk with you through the reality of the consequences. However, God's grace is not a license to be unwise, nor will it magically prevent the natural and negative outcomes of our poor choices.

After Peyton passed, I struggled a lot with anger. Deeply frustrated by the loss of my daughter, my frustration manifested in different ways. One evening I was building some frames in my father-in-law's workshop. Things weren't going right, and I made several mistakes that should have been avoided. In my anger, I lashed out.

Wood splintered as it flew across the workbench. Furious words sailed out of my mouth and echoed off the shop walls. I broke things, and I am not proud of what I did. My anger in that moment was rooted in my pain. My response to my pain broke something that I had originally intended to build. I gazed at the pieces of wood strewn about the workshop and began to calm down.

Suddenly, a warm presence filled the room. Everything that I had broken in my fit of rage supernaturally reassembled itself in front of my very eyes. The pieces floated up off the floor and formed into the frame I originally intended to build. I stood in awe as I watched God clean up the mess I made.

Not really. The splintered pieces of wood lay exactly where they had landed moments before. I had made a mess and it was time to clean it up. Grateful for second chances, I got back to work and completed my project.

We have to live with the consequences of the choices we make when we are in this valley.

I know God loved me through that raw moment in the workshop. I also know that my response was my responsibility. What we do in difficult times matters more than we know. To suffer well, you must cherish your choice and use it wisely. When you do, the strength that remains in you will be channeled into choices that help you. You don't have to make things harder than they already are. By God's grace, you can steward your difficult seasons in a way that leads to life after loss.

WORKBOOK

Chapter Nine Questions

Question: What does it mean to steward your suffering? How can you gauge whether or not you are utilizing this stewardship wisely?

_____

_____

_____

_____

_____

_____

_____

_____

_____

_____

_____

Question: What are some of the messes that often accompany a season of suffering? What are some healthy outlets for the strong emotions brought on by suffering?

_____

_____

_____

_____

_____

_____

_____

_____

_____

_____

Action: Try a new activity or opportunity that will give you a healthy release of anger/grief and empower you to choose to do right in the valley.

Chapter Nine Notes

CHAPTER TEN

The Second Mile: Avoiding Loss After Loss

Walking the various paths through the Three Mile Valley has taken its toll on me and my family. The Temporary, Sustained, Secret, and Tragic paths are all difficult to navigate. We have encountered temporary and sustained seasons of physical infirmities. The heartache of Peyton's passing authored undeniable depression in me. When I share our story in churches, people often approach me and tell me how strong they think I am. While I appreciate their encouragement, I do have to set the record straight with them. I am not as strong as they think I am! My marriage is strong today only by the grace of God. My children still turn to Jesus in prayer every evening by the grace of God. My ministry is still moving forward by the grace of God.

Has God done all the work in the equation of my life? No. I have done my very best to play my part. In order for Him to infuse abundant life in me, God chooses to work cooperatively with me. Remember the equation that I shared at the beginning of the book:

God's Presence + Your Faith Response = Abundant Life

When you cherish your choice, you respond wisely to the difficulty of the Three Mile Valley. Suffering on every level is a loss. But the details do not matter as much as your response to the devastation and disappointment matters. When your dream disappears in an instant in front of you, it is just plain hard. It is critical that you make wise decisions in your pain, because when you don't, you risk authoring additional loss and suffering in your life. Simply put, what you do now influences your next. The future that Jesus is authoring for you is good. You owe it to yourself and to your loved ones to experience it in its fullness.

Disappointment is a part of life. You and I must learn to manage these kinds of moments because our actions will shape the next steps that we take. I have discovered that mismanaged disappointment can lead to debilitating disillusionment. When disillusionment advances in your life, your soul loses its ability to see clearly. The very things to which you had held as absolute truth disappear because you've begun to lose your focus. Your perspective becomes unproductive, and you begin to lose your bearings. Persevering through pain becomes increasingly difficult, because your vision in the valley is compromised.

Debilitating disillusionment can next lead to desperate discouragement. An unproductive perspective prevents perseverance in our lives. As discouragement sets in, your soul loses its strength to fight. This is a key moment in the process. If you're not careful, you can stop protecting the very things you love the most. Your health, relationships, profession, and future are in danger. It has been said that fatigue will make cowards out of us all. No one is immune to the overwhelming power of discouragement.

Desperate discouragement ultimately leads to destructive discontentment. There is such a thing as constructive discontentment, and it is not necessarily bad. For example, a constructive discontentment drives you to improve your health. You know you could be living better, so you want to make a change. However, destructive discontentment is different in a very big way. When you lose focus on what matters and begin to tire, you start believing things that are not true. Living a destructively discontented life is dangerous because of what it creates in us. We cannot afford to let life "dis" us into further loss and heartache.

A while back I was in a conversation with a good friend who shared a profound insight with me. We were discussing the destructive decisions that another person was making. We were heartbroken over the devastation that was happening as a result of his choices. I asked *Why would he ever think that was okay to do?* My friend pondered this question for a moment and then replied, *"Discontentment leads to entitlement."* Let that sink in for a moment.

Destructive discontentment doesn't stay put in our soul. It moves us into illegitimate entitlement. Legitimate entitlement is good. For example, going to work and feeling entitled to the pay you earn is legitimate entitlement. You should get paid because you earned your wage. When an illegitimate entitlement mindset takes root in us, though, we begin to think differently—and destructively. False thoughts, when allowed to linger, will lead us down a path that we don't want to tread. Here are some examples of false thinking in the Three Mile Valley:

- I have lost everything.
- He/she owes me.
- I will never be happy again.
- I no longer have purpose.
- I can't make it without (whatever or whoever you lost).
- I am nothing without (whatever or whoever you lost).
- I can't forgive myself.
- I can't forgive them.

Let me be clear. It is not wrong to think these thoughts. I have wrestled with each of these ideas many times. You will go through the full spectrum of grief as you cope with suffering. That is okay, and you should not feel guilty for that. It is also okay for you to break free from the dangerous cycle that these thoughts can create. You owe it to yourself to think true thoughts in the Three Mile Valley. That is the essence of your journey through the first mile. When you think right, you will do right. This is the essence of the second mile.

When you don't stop the slide that illegitimate entitlement thinking creates, you will descend into unbridled justification. Unbridled justification takes place when Biblical logic leaves the inner discourse you are having with yourself. When you slide into this level of justification, you will find yourself doing things that you said you would never do. All that you once considered wrong has now become right. This is the point at which so many people walking through the Three Mile Valley create additional pain and loss for themselves.

This slide is dangerous, and it should be avoided at all costs. Thankfully, God's grace is present at each stage, ready to help you turn the right way toward abundant life. Here is a quick review of the steps we have just walked through:

Mismanaged disappointment

Debilitating disillusionment

Desperate discouragement

Destructive discontentment

Illegitimate entitlement

Unbridled justification

If you're suffering, understand that you've already lost enough. You don't have to lose any more. You can choose wisely in the middle of your pain. It may not be easy, but because of Jesus it *is* possible. Take a moment to inventory all that you still have left in your life. Name every person who is still walking with you. Identify every good thing that still remains. Count your blessings, one by one. Count your blessings until you're done! When you have listed all that is still right in your world, even if it feels like everything has gone wrong, you can better manage your disappointment and stop the slippery slide that is so easy to experience.

You can avoid mismanaging disappointment, debilitating disillusionment, desperate discouragement, and destructive discontentment. You don't deserve to get "dis'd" by your pain any more. When you cherish your choice as you suffer, you can avoid the illegitimate entitlement that would surely ravage the good things you still have left in your life.

Managing your disappointment will help you maintain a productive perspective. Knowing that now is not forever will change your response to the pain you experience in your life. Commit to making wise decisions when you are still in the Three Mile Valley.

Don't make permanent decisions in temporary seasons.

Managing your disappointment is not always easy, but it is possible. You can avoid the "dis" slide by cultivating contentment in your circumstances. A well-known verse in Philippians speaks to the power of contentment in all of our circumstances:

> *...for I have learned to be content whatever the circumstances. I know what it is to be in need, and I know what it is to have plenty. I have learned the secret of being content in any and every situation, whether well fed or hungry, whether living in plenty or in want. I can do all this through him who gives me strength.*
> **—Philippians 4:11b–13** *(NIV)*

You will benefit immensely when you manage your disappointments. It puts you on a path toward contentment, which is key to suffering well. This makes you unstoppable in every circumstance. When you manage your disappointments, you see your situation more clearly and cultivate a productive perspective. This is what "going pro" in your thought life looks like. Because you remember that you are more than a conqueror in Christ, your productive perspective then fosters increasing encouragement for your soul. This doesn't mean that your situation gets easier; it simply means that you get stronger. Your conqueror DNA is activated, and you begin to discover that what was intended to destroy you is being repurposed for your good. This powerful truth now drives you forward. This strength in your soul is the fuel you need to cultivate contentment in your life.

The first step to cultivating contentment in your life is to declare that truth that Christ is enough. When you meditate on this reality each and every day, you align your mind with the truth. In any and every circumstance, you need to hold fast to the truth that Christ is enough. As you do, you break free from circumstantial living and abide in providential power. Christ-centered contentment creates gospel-driven empowerment. This is the "I can do all things through Christ" reality that contentment secures for us. Because Christ is all we need, we are driven to do more with what we have in our lives instead of waiting on the world to change before we act. The beautiful outcome of gospel-centered empowerment is abundant life in us, as it flows through us. Seasons of suffering can knock you down momentarily as you seek to find your bearings in the storms of life. But because Jesus is present, you don't have to stay down. You can rise and even thrive through your most painful experiences.

The benefits of contentment in your life cannot be overstated. Let's quickly review the steps that you take when you manage disappointment well (read bottom-up):

Abundant Life Through Us

Gospel-Driven Empowerment

Christ-Centered Contentment

Increasing Encouragement

Productive Perspective

Managed Disappointment

Managing your disappointment is key to doing right in the Three Mile Valley. Because of Jesus, you are no longer at the mercy of your circumstances. You now walk with the One who reigns sovereign over your circumstances. God wants the best for you, and He will not be denied by the difficulties that derail you. No, instead your worst day will pale in comparison with the abundant life that you can experience along the way.

As I have said before (and it bears repeating), you have already lost enough. You don't need to lose any more! Cascading seasons of suffering don't have to happen as a result of your current season of suffering. The plan of God is to fully redeem your path through the Three Mile Valley. His commitment to you is unshakable, and the abundant life He is resurrecting in you is unstoppable. When you cherish your choice, you not only avoid loss after loss, but you also position yourself to actually *gain* through your loss.

WORKBOOK

Chapter Ten Questions

Question: Have you ever added to a season of suffering by making poor choices? What were the consequences of these choices? How could you have made better choices?

_____

_____

_____

_____

_____

_____

_____

_____

_____

_____

_____

Question: What is a disappointment that you are struggling with in your current suffering? How can you manage it so it doesn't "dis" you?

_____

_____

_____

_____

_____

_____

_____

_____

_____

_____

Action: As you reflect on your current season of suffering, identify a concrete action you can take to further your journey through each of the six steps to managing disappointment well. For each step, also choose and write out a relevant scripture to post in a place where you will see it daily—as a reminder and encouragement to you through your season of suffering.

Chapter Ten Notes

CHAPTER ELEVEN

The Second Mile: Grace in the Fire

I have pleaded with God to take away my family's pain and suffering on each of the paths we have walked. Instead of answering my prayer the way I'd hoped, however, God gave me something different. He gave me grace. The apostle Paul illustrates the ways in which God will sometimes answer our cries for relief with something else.

> *Three times I pleaded with the Lord to take it away from me. But he said to me, "My grace is sufficient for you, for my power is made perfect in weakness." Therefore I will boast all the more gladly about my weaknesses, so that Christ's power may rest on me. That is why, for Christ's sake, I delight in weaknesses, in insults, in hardships, in persecutions, in difficulties. For when I am weak, then I am strong.*
>
> **—2 Corinthians 12:8–10** (NIV)

Many verses in the Bible seem to insult my sensibilities and upend my view of God. This passage is one of them! In response to our pain, God gives us His presence (Psalm 34:8). He gives us what we need, but He does not always give us what we want. Instead of altering our circumstances, God's first response is to alter us in our circumstances by infusing us with His grace.

His grace goes to work in us as He lovingly works out our circumstances around us. Perfecting us from the inside out is God's primary plan. If you're like me, you would like God to first make the world around us perfect before working on the inside.

Quite often, God uses people around us to show us what we need to know. In my journey, I have discovered that a message reaches a mind, but a story reaches a soul. Truthful information is good. Truthful incarnation is better. The story that God is writing through you is more powerful than you know. For more than fifteen years, I have watched God's power and presence manifest itself through a certain person He placed in my life. Let me tell you a little more about the most amazing woman I have ever met.

My wife is amazing. I figured this out soon after I met her. Our friendship started with a game of one-on-one basketball. Who won? I would rather not talk about it. Not only is she a good basketball player, but she is a true friend to everyone. She has always been this way.

Her first day of school underscores her passion for people. The teacher stepped out of the classroom for a minute.

While everyone waited for the teacher to return, Marlena saw an opportunity.

This confident blond-haired ball of energy left her seat and walked right up to the front of the classroom. "Raise your hand if you would like to be my friend," she instructed her fellow students. Sure enough, every kid in the classroom raised their hand. Marlena made sure everyone who wanted a friend that day had one in her.

Her sincere love for people is one of the reasons I fell in love with her. We married with one year left in college, and we never looked back. Throughout the course of our marriage, I have watched my bride navigate some challenging seasons. One of these seasons occurred rather recently for us.

This next part sounds like a joke: Marlena started having severe migraines after she married me. But it wasn't a laughing matter.

The headaches would happen every month and would last a few days. If you have ever had a migraine, you understand her pain. Her headaches were so intense that they would drive her into the darkness of our bedroom, with the windows blacked out and plenty of pillows available to dampen the noise.

But since our college days, the headaches have progressed. They began happening more often and lasting longer when they hit her.

In the thirteenth year of our marriage, we entered a season of sustained suffering. And this particular valley introduced us to the most severe run of headaches Marlena had ever experienced. That November and December, she sheltered herself in a darkened bedroom for forty-five days out of sixty.

The headaches began occurring even more frequently in January of the following year. When they claimed six days out of every week, we felt helpless. Everything we tried failed to provide relief. January and February were terribly challenging for Marlena. By March, we were all exhausted by the sheer gravity that chronic illness creates. Thankfully, Marlena finally began to experience some relief from her headaches as the spring progressed.

By the end of that year, Marlena's headaches retreated to claiming between twenty and twenty-five days every month. I am happy to tell you that as I write this book that she has improved even more. A typical month now gives her ten to fifteen days of severe migraines.

We believe that God is working to restore Marlena to full health. Until He does, however, we are committed to suffering well and cherishing our choice in this valley.

You might be wondering how my wife is able to survive these headaches. The answer is that she controls what she can. When she is in pain, she chooses to listen to uplifting music and read passages of Scripture. When she is able, she also watches her favorite shows, reads avidly, and journals about her experiences. Although she is regularly sidelined for days at a stretch, she knows that the headache will eventually lift. And when it does, she is up and out of the house, committed to living as much life as she can. She hangs out with friends, goes shopping, and attends church services. Knowing that a headache-free day will soon come doesn't make her pain any less, but it does empower her to focus on what she can control while the headache is still present.

Watching Marlena navigate this season of suffering has been amazing. She has decided to cherish her choice. While she is unable to control the fact that she has headaches, she is controlling what she can. She is my picture of what it means to have grace in the fire. This is the essence of the second mile.

What if God's doesn't answer our prayers for Marlena's complete healing? Lord knows, we have asked a thousand times. We do believe that it is only a matter of time before she will be completely free from the headaches that have taken so much from her. But until He does, we control what we can, cherish our choice, and trust in His presence to see us through.

In your own valley, it is important to remember that God is present. His presence promises provision in the pain. When we focus on Him, and not what we expect Him to do for us, we will never be disappointed.

God may come through exactly the way you pray He does. When that happens, celebrate and tell the world. Or God may choose a different response to your prayers. When that happens, celebrate and tell the world.

We hope in God because He is greater than His ability to save us from pain. He is so much greater, in fact, that He sustains us in our pain. His power is what propels us through the deepest heartache and the most unimaginable disappointments.

We follow Jesus because of who He is, not what He does for us. He never promised us a pain-free life. He promised us abundant life in our pain. This truth empowers us to cherish our choice. It fuels us to live with grace in the fire. You don't have to let life happen to you anymore. Yes, there will be circumstances that you cannot control. But because of Jesus, you can cherish your choice by controlling what you can as you live with grace in the fire.

WORKBOOK

Chapter Eleven Questions

Question: As you go through your valley of suffering, what are you able to control?

_____

_____

_____

_____

_____

_____

_____

_____

_____

_____

_____

Question: Are you committed to following Jesus even if He does not fix your situation or answer your prayers in the way you desire? How would you describe your commitment to Him?

_____

_____

_____

_____

_____

_____

_____

_____

_____

_____

_____

Action: In your study group or with a Christian friend, share two prayers that God has answered recently—one that He answered in the way you desired and one that He answered in a way you did not prefer. What did you learn from each situation?

Chapter Eleven Notes

CHAPTER TWELVE

The Second Mile: Mind Your Meds

I had a crush when I was in the eighth grade, long before I met Marlena. My eighth-grade crush had beautiful eyes and curly blond hair. Growing up in Minnesota, I was mesmerized by her Southern accent. Everything she said was pure magic. I was smitten.

Things in our relationship came to a crossroads on a day when I was playing a game of pickup basketball at the local gym. This game had a significantly different outcome than the game I found myself playing against Marlena many years later. Let me be clear: I was not a good basketball player by any means. However, my crush was there, and so it was my time to become an amazing basketball player.

At one point during the game, I was driving into the lane for a layup. As I jumped, my feet tangled with another player's. I rotated midair and fell flat onto my back.

Searing pain shot down both of my legs, and it felt like I had been hit with a baseball bat right in my lower back.

I struggled to get up. I struggled to walk. Yet somehow, I managed to keep playing. Why? My crush was watching!

I remember hearing the diagnosis from my doctor: I sat there in disbelief as he told me I had herniated a disc during my fall on the basketball court. The damaged disc was in the lumbar region of my back. It required surgery.

When I woke up in the recovery room after the procedure, my doctor just about came unglued when I told him that I couldn't move my legs. Turns out, the medication they had given me was so powerful that it had disconnected me from reality. I honestly believed that I was paralyzed. You can imagine my doctor's relief when I eventually began to wiggle my toes without any problem.

Shortly after, the nursing staff relocated me to my long-term room. Within minutes of my arrival, my hockey team showed up. I was in no shape to entertain, but boy, did I entertain that day. The medication in my system set the stage for what happened next.

The phone rang in my room. I reached to answer it. I held the phone up to my ear and said, "Hello?" To this day, I cannot remember who called. I do remember what I said, though. With the entire hockey team watching, I told the caller that we would be playing a game—that afternoon! I have to laugh as I think about that moment now. I know my teammates did.

Medication is powerful stuff. As you walk through the Three Mile Valley you need to mind your meds carefully. I am not just talking about the little pills you get from the pharmacy. I am talking about all the numerous different ways you and I cope with tough times.

Everyone self-medicates in some way—in other words, we are all prone to turning to a myriad of things to numb the pain of our circumstances. This isn't always a bad thing, but it can become unhealthy if what you are turning to is just masking symptoms and isn't truly helping you heal.

For most of us, it isn't a question of whether or not we will medicate; it is a question of how we will medicate. This is important because some medications help us to heal, and others delay our healing. As we suffer well through the Three Mile Valley, we need to choose our medications wisely.

Three healthy "medications" can help you manage your pain as you walk through your particular valley.

The Presence of God

The first medication that God provides is His loving presence.

> *Not only so, but we also glory in our sufferings, because we know that suffering produces perseverance; perseverance, character; and character, hope. And hope does not put us to shame, because God's love has been poured out into our hearts through the Holy Spirit, who has been given to us.*
> *—Romans 5:3–5 (NIV)*

God pushes a dose of help your way every single day. It is poured out into your heart through the Holy Spirit.

This heavenly love is unlike anything we can find here on earth. It is pure and powerful. It is free and full of life.

God's presence doesn't make our suffering any easier. But when we rest in God's presence, we can see that suffering is one of the ways that God makes us stronger. In response to the pain, God gives us a hope that will not put us to shame.

To take this divine dose of medication, all you need to do is pray. His presence is like an omnipresent wi-fi network, and Jesus is the password. Prayer logs you on to His network and allows for a download of strength to happen as you upload your cares.

The Word of God

The second medication that God supplies is His Word. The Bible is not just *a* good book; it is *the* God Book. It is more than print on paper and sentences on the screen of your digital device.

Take a look at Romans 15:4 (NIV). It says, "For everything that was written in the past was written to teach us, so that through the endurance taught in the Scriptures and the encouragement they provide we might have hope."

When you and I study the Bible, we learn endurance and receive encouragement. This prescription is predestined by God to give us hope. You are set yourself up for success when you read the Word of God.

Your word is a lamp for my feet, a light on my path.
—Psalm 119:105 *(NIV)*

God's Word is a guiding light for everyday life. It illuminates our way through the Three Mile Valley just enough to help us see our next step.

God's Word is full of promises that apply to our particular path. When you know what God can do, it isn't a matter of *if* He will, but *when* He will.

Let the Word of God illuminate each step you take through your difficult seasons. You will be more capable of stepping wisely as you steward your season of suffering. You will have help to see more of what is happening around you because the Bible is a lamp for your feet.

> *You never have to hold God to His promises.*
> *You only have to hold fast within them.*

For the word of God is alive and active. Sharper than any double-edged sword, it penetrates even to dividing soul and spirit, joints and marrow; it judges the thoughts and attitudes of the heart.
—Hebrews 4:12 (NIV)

In addition to illuminating our circumstances, the Word of God is also penetrating. It cuts past our façades and gets to the heart of every matter. It introduces us to God's thoughts in ways that would otherwise be unattainable. It shows us our true reflection as we gaze into the mirror of its counsel.

Take the helmet of salvation and the sword of the Spirit,
which is the word of God.
                                    —Ephesians 6:17 *(NIV)*

There are going to be stretches of your valley that will require you to fight. The Word of God is the only offensive weapon we have for the battle. You will need to have your sword ready to cut down the lies of your spiritual enemy, the devil. You will be equipped to suffer well when you walk with God's Word hidden in your heart. Arm yourself, because the battle will be intense. Encourage yourself, because you will win when you stand on God's Word.

Take this dose of medication by reading the Bible regularly. Read it in the valley. Heck, read it outside of the valley. You will find God's grace preparing you for what lies ahead, so you can carry it with you in difficult times.

The People of God

The third medication that God gives us is His Church. Having a team is key to winning in every season. The Church is your God-given team. Your "weekly huddle" may include twenty people or twenty-five thousand. Regardless of the size of the church, it is critical that you faithfully and regularly participate.

And let us consider how we may spur one another on to-
ward love and good deeds, not giving up meeting together,
as some are in the habit of doing, but encouraging one an-
other—and all the more as you see the Day approaching.
                              —Hebrews 10:24–25 *(NIV)*

Too often we stop doing the things we need to do when life gets hard. Going to church is no exception. You cannot afford to stop attending church when you are walking through the Three Mile Valley; there is too much at stake. Take a dose of this medication often. Your presence in the body of Christ is the prescription for your soul.

Every time you show up, you give God a chance to show off. He wants to show you that you are not alone. He wants to show others in the body of Christ that suffering is a normal part of carrying one's cross. This mutual edification brings authenticity to His Church.

Something powerful happens when we all know that we are not okay, but that it will all be okay. When you gather with others to worship, hear the teaching of the Word, and connect with each other, you receive a healthy dose of medication for your journey.

Other Medications

There are other medications that are safe for you to rely on as you journey through the Three Mile Valley. Listen to the needs of your heart and body and take these things in moderation so they don't become unhealthy addictions or obsessions. Here are a few of them:

- Exercise
- Laughter
- Sleep
- Friendship
- Healthy food
- Work

Take each of these medications in addition to the presence of God, the Word of God, and the Church of God. When you mind your meds, you set yourself up to suffer well.

These medications are beneficial for your soul, even when you are not going through any difficulty. The medications you rely on outside of the valley will be the same medications you turn to while in the valley; if you typically rely on unhealthy medications, this will only escalate when you face difficult times.

You owe it to yourself to medicate wisely in every season of life. When you do, you allow ample room for the abundant life of Christ to fill every part of your soul. This abundant life inside of you is greater than anything you face outside of you.

WORKBOOK

Chapter Twelve Questions

Question: What are some helpful and some unhelpful ways that people seek to soothe their pain in the midst of suffering? Which of these "meds" have you used, and what were the results?

_____

_____

_____

_____

_____

_____

_____

_____

_____

_____

_____

Question: How have the presence of God, the Word of God, and the church of God brought you comfort in the valley of suffering?

_____

_____

_____

_____

_____

_____

_____

_____

_____

_____

Action: Ask a trusted friend if there are any areas of "self-medicating" in which you are off balance (e.g., working to exhaustion, over- or under-sleeping, over- or undereating). Prayerfully consider any blind spots your friend points out, and ask for accountability to use these "meds" in a healthy and balanced way.

Chapter Twelve Notes

_____

_____

_____

_____

_____

_____

_____

_____

_____

_____

_____

_____

_____

_____

_____

_____

_____

_____

_____

CHAPTER THIRTEEN

The Second Mile:
Soul Rehab

After my back surgery, I went through a rehabilitation process. Learning how to live with pain as I progressed toward wholeness was not easy. My doctor told me to start doing the rehab exercises as soon as I was able. Waiting until all my pain was gone was not an option. It was time for me to start building a life on the other side of my injury. I was nowhere close to healed when the rehab process began. Some of the exercises were painful to do, but necessary if I wanted to recover completely.

The rehab process was incredibly important because it impacted the rest of my life. I am living an active life today because of the choices I made in response to an injury I experienced in eighth grade.

How you and I steward the space and time between our loss and this moment directly impacts our healing. Our response in the valleys of life will either hasten or inhibit our healing. God desires for you to be healed. When you cherish your choice, you hasten your healing. When you rehab your soul, you are giving God the time and space to heal you.

Time Heals Nothing

You have probably heard people say that "time heals all wounds." In my own journey through the Three Mile Valley, I have discovered this to be false. Time possesses no magical power to heal any wound. The power that time does possess, however, creates space between the point of pain and your present reality. If we expect time alone to heal our wounded souls, we will be waiting forever. There are concrete actions you can take to hasten your healing.

Your response to the adversity you face is important. God will do His part. He will author good things from the setbacks you endure. However, He is only part of the equation. Remember the Three Mile Valley equation from earlier in this book?

God's Presence + Your Faith Response = Abundant Life

Pain's power is quite persuasive. It tempts you to stay put until the pain subsides. While this is wise in some scenarios, it is not the best choice in every situation. The reason why is that the only thing stopped permanently as I wait for the pain to stop is me—life goes on.

To gain the advantage over your pain, all you need to do is put it into perspective. In Christ, you are permanent;

your pain is not. Your season is temporary; you are not. Make decisions that shape a future you can thrive in, not ones that only apply to your temporary season.

Rehab Exercises

There are four exercises you need to do as you journey through the Three Mile Valley. They are meant to be done regularly and at your own pace—albeit steadily.

Exercise Faith

God doesn't need us to trust Him in order to be God. But we need to trust Him in order to experience Him as God.

> *Trust in the LORD with all your heart and lean not on your own understanding; in all your ways submit to him, and he will make your paths straight.*
> **—Proverbs 3:5–6** *(NIV)*

As you walk through your valley, remember the promise found in this verse. God makes our path navigable when we trust Him, even when we don't understand.

Recently I flew to Vietnam with some friends. Our first flight was fourteen hours or so. It made our second flight, which was five hours, seem like a walk in the park.

I remember sitting on the fourteen-hour flight and being struck by a thought. While I was sitting there, essentially waiting, we were still moving—and quite fast, I might add.

On that flight, I placed my trust in the pilot, and he rewarded my trust. The entire time I was seated, the pilot was making sure I was headed in the right direction. What felt like waiting was actually getting me to where I needed to be.

The same is true for us as we "wait" in our seasons of suffering. When we trust the Lord, He works to get us where we need to be in ways that we could not do on our own.

While you are waiting, God is working.

But they who wait for the LORD shall renew their strength; they shall mount up with wings like eagles; they shall run and not be weary; they shall walk and not faint.
—Isaiah 40:31 (ESV)

When it feels like your faith in God has you sitting in a waiting room instead of walking forward on a path, it is okay. When you and I trust Him above everything else, we can be sure that everything will eventually work out. Faith is not always an easy exercise, but it always brings us results we can live with.

Exercise Forward

The best way through the Three Mile Valley is forward. Why? Because now is not forever and this earth is not our eternal home. Take a look at what the apostle Paul says in the following verse.

> *I press on toward the goal to win the prize for which God has called me heavenward in Christ Jesus.*
> **—Philippians 3:14** *(NIV)*

When you and I suffer well, we set our sights on heaven even as we walk through hell on earth. We are passing through this space because it is not our permanent resting place. Commit to moving forward, knowing you can never go back to the life you had outside the Three Mile Valley. When you do emerge from the valley, you will be different. Your world will be different. There is an abundantly ever after waiting for you because Jesus is working in you now. Every step you take forward brings you that much closer to the good that God is working through your seasons of suffering.

Every year following the loss of our daughter, we do this exercise as a family. It is an important part of rehab for our wounded souls. We take a trip on the anniversary of Peyton's passing. We go somewhere fun to make good memories on the date that will forever be full of painful ones.

To date, we have visited Disney World, Disneyland, and the Wisconsin Dells, and we have even taken a Disney cruise. Is it a coincidence that we regularly visit the "happiest place on earth" on the worst date on our calendar? I think not.

This exercise is one way we declare that we will continue to live through our pain. It has been both intensely difficult and powerfully rewarding. Those who are grieving the loss of a loved one should not read this to mean that you should "get over it." Grief is a journey that will lead you through multiple stages. While there is a typical order, it is common for those in grief to jump between stages and even return to stages of grief more than once. We will never get over Peyton's passing, and we shouldn't. Instead, we will carry her memory forward with us as we heal along the way.

As you suffer well through your valley, exercise forward. It is one way you can cherish your choice and steward your season of suffering with wisdom. God is not done writing your story. You will live even through loss, heartache, setback, and suffering. Resolve today to suffer well and move forward at your pace.

Exercise Forgiveness

Forgiveness is a key exercise you must perform if you want to suffer well through the Three Mile Valley. It is also a mandate for everyone who follows Jesus.

> *For if you forgive other people when they sin against you, your heavenly Father will also forgive you. But if you do not forgive others their sins, your Father will not forgive your sins.*
>
> *—Matthew 6:14–15* (NIV)

Matthew 6:14 minces nothing as Jesus lays out the need for us to exercise forgiveness. You *must* forgive others if you want God to forgive you.

When you accept Jesus' invitation to follow Him, you drop your way in order to go His way. When you refuse to forgive others for the ways in which they wrong you, you are walking your way. It is a path away from Jesus, and you risk losing more than you could ever imagine.

Unforgiveness is the opposite of all that Jesus is about. His way is forgiveness for all people and for everything they have done. He liberally offers forgiveness to everyone who asks. The one who walks in His way is a primary benefactor of unreasonable grace on every level.

> *Your right to hurt someone in return for how they have hurt you is surrendered when you forgive. Your freedom from bitterness is gained when you forgive.*

Bitterness is the unruly companion of the unforgiving heart. It takes up residence and seeps into every corner of our lives. When you activate the power of forgiveness, you sever the dark power of bitterness over your life.

Your path through the Three Mile Valley might be full of pain caused by the choices of another. In that case, this exercise in forgiveness could be difficult for you.

Invite Jesus into your pain and ask Him for help. Your confession of faith will usher grace directly into your soul. When you admit your need, you receive the help of heaven. God wants you to walk in forgiveness, and He will provide everything you need to take each step.

Exercising forgiveness in the Three Mile Valley lightens your load exponentially. When you shed the excess weight of a bitter heart, you gain so much. You find freedom for every step that lies ahead.

Exercise Self-Forgetfulness

Serving others as you journey through the Three Mile Valley is counterintuitive. Quite often, God's ideas are.

> *Do nothing from selfish ambition or conceit, but in humility count others more significant than yourselves. Let each of you look not only to his own interests, but also to the interests of others.*
>
> **—Philippians 2:3–4** (ESV)

We have been blessed to have great friends for our entire married life. For several years, we watched two of our good friends struggle to get pregnant. Our hearts broke for Gabe and Serah as they journeyed on the sustained path through the Three Mile Valley.

Shortly after Peyton's passing, we got the news that their twins were born. You read that right: twins. Marlena and I decided to go and visit our friends and experience their doubly blessed reality for ourselves. We are so glad we did so, too—their twin babies were adorable! As is the custom, we brought gifts for our friends to celebrate their growing family.

Why did we do that? We had every reason to stay cocooned in our pain. No one would have judged us if we had chosen to stay away. However, something inside of us compelled us to make the trip. Questions swirled through my mind as I thought through our visit beforehand. The most frightening question I wrestled with was, *Will the sight of a newborn remind us of our Peyton? How will I respond if it does?* Those questions were fueled by fear, which did not want us reaching past our pain to bless someone else.

It was not easy to exercise self-forgetfulness, but when we did so, it was liberating. Although we went to give to our friends, we received so much more in return.

God's promise to you in the valley is clear. When you lift your eyes up and off of your situation and serve those around you, your world is illuminated. Self-forgetfulness is the call of the cross in every season of life.

The benefit of service during your suffering is life-changing. Specifically, your life will change as you seek to help others change their lives. Exercising self-forgetfulness is key to suffering well through the Three Mile Valley.

Rehab Well

To suffer well you need to rehab well. As you walk through the Three Mile Valley remember to cherish your choice and steward your season well. Your healing is on the way. Your soul can be made well when you exercise faith, forward movement, forgiveness, and self-forgetfulness.

Chapter Thirteen Questions

Question: What is an example of a permanent choice someone might make in a temporary season? Why is this unwise? How can you be sure the Lord is guiding your decisions in the valley?

_____

_____

_____

_____

_____

_____

_____

_____

_____

_____

_____

Question: Faith, Forward, Forgiveness, and Self-forget-fulness: Which rehab exercise is the easiest for you? Which is the hardest? Why?

_____

_____

_____

_____

_____

_____

_____

_____

_____

_____

_____

Action: What is a tangible decision you can make to "exercise forward"? Or to "exercise self-forgetfulness" in ministering to someone else (perhaps even the person for whom you have been praying)? Begin planning or acting on this decision this week.

Chapter Thirteen Notes

SECOND MILE RECAP

Remember, Cherish Your Choice

Doing right is key to conquering the second mile of the Three Mile Valley. No one else can respond to your suffering for you, and it is up to you to steward this season of suffering well. As you live with grace in the fire, commit to controlling what you can. Medicate wisely and embrace the process your soul needs to rehab. This is the point at which God's sovereignty and your personal responsibility intersect. When you do right in the Three Mile Valley, you will continue to suffer well.

Declarations to Help You Steward Your Suffering:

- My response is my responsibility.
- I will respond wisely to pain, because I take the messes I make with me.

- I will not make permanent choices in temporary seasons.
- I will medicate wisely through difficult seasons.
- I will trust God because I know that while I am waiting, God is working.
- I will not live in the past; I will press on toward the goal.
- I will forgive those who do me wrong because Jesus has forgiven me first.
- I will surrender my right to exact revenge on those who have done me wrong.
- I will serve others as I am able.

CHAPTER FOURTEEN

The Third Mile:
There Is Always an After

You've made it to the third mile of our journey! The third mile welcomes us with hopeful signs of life and renewal. If the first and second miles are about what you can do, the third mile is about what God is already doing on your behalf. Watching God make everything all right is the key to conquering this mile.

Losing our daughter suddenly at thirteen months has taught us much. One of the biggest lessons is that God is working it all out. His goodness to us guarantees that there is always an after.

And we know that God causes everything to work together for the good of those who love God and are called according to his purpose for them.
—**Romans 8:28** *(NLT)*

There's a saying that goes, "Everything will be okay in the end. If it's not okay, it's not the end." This thought captures the essence of perspective. We are people of faith who trust in the One who is greater than everything we face. When we suffer well, we live knowing that everything will eventually be okay. This brings us to our third and final principle.

There is Always an After—Watch God Make It All Right

God is the master of the after. He alone sits above time as He simultaneously walks with us right now. His perspective gives Him the ability to see well beyond this moment. As God looks forward, He sees all that He can accomplish through your darkest times. He is authoring an after that is abundant in nature and far beyond anything we could shape on our own. The first, and the most amazing after, is eternity in heaven. The gospel gives us an amazing hope. Jesus accomplished what we couldn't to give us what we can't live without. Before He ascended to heaven, Jesus gave us this promise:

> *"Do not let your hearts be troubled. You believe in God; believe also in me. My Father's house has many rooms; if that were not so, would I have told you that I am going there to prepare a place for you? And if I go and prepare a place for you, I will come back and take you to be with me that you also may be where I am. You know the way to the place where I am going."*
> *—John 14:1–4 (NIV)*

The hope of heaven is the best after we can have. There, we will discover all of the preparations Jesus made for our arrival. This place is waiting for us and will be abundantly better than the life we have now. It brings great comfort to us to know that Jesus prepared a place for Peyton long before she passed away. The after that Jesus created for her is beyond our wildest imagination. It is a good place, where her soul experiences God's fullness in ways we simply cannot comprehend.

Because of Jesus, Marlena and I will also experience this after. Whenever we should pass through the veil of eternity, we will be welcomed into an after that we did not earn or deserve. All the suffering we have experienced in this life will cease in heaven.

> *God will wipe away every tear from their eyes; there shall*
> *be no more death, nor sorrow, nor crying. There shall be*
> *no more pain, for the former things have passed away.*
>
> **—Revelation 21:4** *(NKJV)*

Heaven is the first after that we can look forward to as we journey through the Three Mile Valley. It is guaranteed to everyone who accepts Jesus' invitation to follow Him. As you walk through the Three Mile Valley, you can know with certainty that the place Jesus has prepared for you is good.

It must be said that some who journey through the Three Mile Valley step into eternity as a result of the suffering they endure in the valley. They receive the fullness of heaven that Jesus promised them, and experience now what you and I can only imagine. If heaven was the only after that God authored for us, that would be more than we deserved. This brings us to another after that God is faithfully working out on our behalf.

God is writing an alternate ending to your story. He has the last word, and it is often revealed after you walk through your darkest days. What He writes is good. Though you may have lost more than you ever imagined, God is undertaking to add something greater within you that no one can take away.

Though the darkness may have swallowed you whole, the light of eternity that burns within will intensify. This is what happens when our God speaks the last word. While life subtracts from you, God is adding to you. He is not stumped by our setbacks, stymied by our suffering, or derailed by death.

God adds through seasons of subtraction.

The beauty of Jesus' story is that it is an example of what God can do in your story.

After He was crucified, the world around Jesus' tomb continued to spin on. The soldiers standing guard outside the grave had no clue they were about to witness a resurrection. You see, the world thought the funeral was final, that the grave had the last word.

Then, after three days had passed, God authored an alternate ending the world was not expecting. The ground began to shake, the stone was rolled away, and our Savior stepped out of the tomb. Death was defanged the moment Jesus came roaring back to life. The Master Valley Walker completed His conquest of the Three Mile Valley and made victory possible for each and every one of us.

This is why the gospel is such good news! It is the proclamation that the Great One has begun to write an alternate ending for our story. It is one that we do not fully deserve, but it is one that we will fully experience!

The paradox of the gospel is death through life. Jesus turns your tomb into a womb. In other words, your sarcophagus becomes a sanctified delivery room. The very place that declares the finality of death transforms into a place of redemptive potential through the cross of Jesus Christ. Abundant new life emerges from abundant death. The hope we have in Jesus holds fast to the promise that whatever Jesus says should live, will live! This is part of the good that God works out through every circumstance for those who love Him.

Not only does our ever-after end well eternally, but there are also times when God advances heaven into earth and gives us an "after" here on earth that is full of joy. When heaven collides with the here and now, we are in the midst of a miracle.

Our "after" story with Peyton is full of God's faithfulness. We regularly witness God use our story to help others walk through their valley. We saw God preserve our family through the most intense portions of our tragic season. The after that we are living reveals the goodness of our God.

Not only has God prepared an eternal home for you in heaven, He is actively bringing heaven to earth through your valley. He is the only one creative and powerful enough to author good through any and every circumstance.

As you complete your journey through the Three Mile Valley, you can know that God is working good through every step you take. Keep reading to discover my family's abundantly ever after and see for yourself how God is authoring abundant life through the Three Mile Valley.

I consider that our present sufferings are not worth comparing with the glory that will be revealed in us.
—Romans 8:18 *(NIV)*

Chapter Fourteen Questions

Question: What is the difference between resolution and redemption? Can there be redemption of suffering without resolution of suffering? Why or why not?

_____

_____

_____

_____

_____

_____

_____

_____

_____

_____

Question: Who do you know who has experienced a beautiful "after" to their season of suffering? How does their story encourage you?

_____

_____

_____

_____

_____

_____

_____

_____

_____

_____

_____

Action: Take a moment to imagine your "after." Can you see a glimpse past the valley to the glory of heaven, to greater ministry on earth, to renewal and redemption and new beginnings? Ask God to renew your hope that there will be a beautiful "after" to your story, and then hold on to that hope in the days ahead.

Chapter Fourteen Notes

CHAPTER FIFTEEN

The Third Mile: Abundantly Ever After

On November 30, 2011, our lives changed. On July 2, 2013, our lives changed again.

We were sound asleep in a camper while on a family vacation. My son, Logan, slept in the bunk above me, and Marlena was in the very narrow bed across from me. She was very pregnant—nine months' pregnant, in fact— so her sleeping in such a small and uncomfortable bed seemed like a cruel joke. When she uttered the following words, however, I was no longer able to sleep: "I think my water just broke."

It sure had! Before anyone else at the campground was awake, we scrambled to get ourselves headed to the hospital. First, we went to our friends' tent next door to ask if they could be with Logan and bring him up to speed when he awoke—check. Second, to the maternity ward just five minutes away.

My nervousness was impossible to hide as I paced outside of the operating room. I was covered from head to toe in blue scrubs, complete with surgical mask. The team of medical professionals calmly moved in and out of the room with the intentionality and precision of a drill team. Every time the door opened, my heart stopped. I waited. And waited. And waited.

The door opened one last time, and a nurse broke the silence, "We're ready for you."

I walked into the large operating room, fully aware of the shoe coverings that gave me sensation of gliding across the floor. I was so excited, I was practically floating! To see my wife ready to deliver our youngest child into the world brought me nearly to tears. Not yet, though. Those would come later. First, the C-section.

I took my place up by her head and grabbed a seat. Apparently, some husbands don't do well with the surgical activities that play out in a C-section. Not this guy! I was fascinated by every bit of it. The curtain stretched vertically across her shoulders, ensuring that Marlena would not be able to see what happened next. I'm not going to lie; I did peek a few times over the curtain out of sheer curiosity.

After some preliminary incisions, the doctors let us know they were getting close to retrieving our daughter. I marvel to this day at Marlena's strength throughout this whole operation. Both of us were awash in the emotion of the moment. We both had died a parent's death the evening Peyton passed. Would this be the moment when God would resurrect our broken hearts?

The room fell suddenly silent. Every eye was focused on the middle of the operating table. The doctor triumphantly raised our newborn daughter. Welcome to the world, Camdyn Joy Herod! After a brief meeting with her momma, she was quickly passed off to the team of nurses who were charged with her care.

After a few moments, the nurses invited me over to the warming table. They wrapped her up with a blanket and handed her over to me. I could not do anything but cry as I held our beautiful gift. My heart soared as it ached.

Camdyn didn't replace Peyton that day. She became Peyton's sister. And every day since has been full of life and loss. This is not the happily-ever-after that we wanted. But by the grace of God, it is the abundantly-ever-after He is authoring through our darkest days.

Does God give happily-ever-afters? I am not sure. Does He give abundantly-ever-afters? Most definitely.

My family has walked the temporary, sustained, secret and tragic paths through Three Mile Valley. By the grace of God, we can live to tell about it. Our marriage is strong. Our children pray at bedtime. Our family is committed to serving Jesus.

Our abundantly ever after is full of joy. While it is not the life we originally intended, it is the best version of the life we have now. God has an abundantly ever after waiting for you as well, and it starts a whole lot sooner than you may think.

WORKBOOK

Chapter Fifteen Questions

Question: What might an abundantly-ever-after look like in your current suffering?

_____

_____

_____

_____

_____

_____

_____

_____

_____

_____

_____

Question: How does the thought of an abundantly-ever-after make you feel? Does it make you feel nervous, excited, like it would be too good to be true? Why?

_____

_____

_____

_____

_____

_____

_____

_____

_____

_____

_____

Action: Write down Bible verses about God's grace and love. Reread them whenever you have doubts about God's willingness to bring abundance and good out of your suffering.

Chapter Fifteen Notes

CHAPTER SIXTEEN

The Third Mile: Your "After" Starts Now

The monarch butterfly is considered by some to be the most beautiful butterfly on the planet. Its name means "king," a meaning that further illustrates its place in the butterfly family. I remember the time when a monarch landed on my knee as it took a momentary break from its flight, the distinct black, orange, and white markings on its wings utterly captivating me. I was silent in my fascinated observation, until, moments later, the butterfly lifted off in a flourish of graceful flight. It was a beautiful moment from start to finish.

That butterfly didn't always look that way, however, and it hadn't always been able to fly. In fact, just weeks earlier it had been a caterpillar, limited to crawling in order to get around. By design, the caterpillar weaves itself into a cocoon. For ten days, everything stands still, from all outward appearances. But don't be deceived by what you see, because there is transformational activity taking place under the surface. The crawling caterpillar ultimately emerges as a butterfly, complete with wings for flight. God designed the monarch's journey to be this way, and it serves as a clear picture for us as we walk through the Three Mile Valley. God is faithful to use every single thing that happens in our lives for our good. I have quoted a particular verse from Romans multiple times in this book, but it is worth revisiting one more time:

And we know that God causes everything to work together for the good of those who love God and are called according to his purpose for them.
—Romans 8:28 (NIV)

In other words, God will not waste your tears, your heartache, or your pain. Much like the monarch butterfly's cocoon, the Three Mile Valley is a place full of transformational activity. Even through the darkness, God is working to orchestrate an after that is good for you. The process is not something we might readily enjoy, but the product fills us with joy!

We want God to transfer us out of our pain.
God wants to transform us through our pain.

The Three Mile Valley is a place you walk through, not a place you will stay. The promise that you have in Christ is that there is always an after on the other side of loss, suffering, setbacks, and disappointment. You can walk through these valleys because heartache is not your home and because destruction is not your destination. Every single thing you face in life has been conquered by your Savior, who will lead you victoriously through every obstacle.

God, in His infinite wisdom and grace, is using the Three Mile Valley for your good. He is faithfully adding to you, even when the unfairness of life seems to only subtract from you.

Too many people fall prey to the thought that they will be fulfilled *someday*. They worship an illegitimate idol that promises a good life *over there*. The problem with this way of thinking is that it lulls us into accepting a quality of life far below the one Jesus has purchased for us. Jesus didn't come to give you a happy life; He came to fill you with abundant life!

The powerful reality of God's kingdom is that it exists in a perpetual state of tension. Jesus declared over and over that it was already here, but not yet arrived. The truth is, your abundantly-ever-after starts the moment you reach up to grab Jesus' hand. As you follow Him, He faithfully brings forth unbelievably good things in the midst of impossibly difficult situations. Yes, you will suffer in this life. There is no question about that. But by the grace of God, you will also abundantly live.

God's presence produces the possibility of your faith response. And your faith response leads to abundant life in Christ every day thereafter. When Jesus enters the picture, abundant life does, too. You are no longer bound by circumstances. You are held in the grip of stronger hands.

Do not wait until you come through your Three Mile Valley to start living your abundantly-ever-after. Reject wholeheartedly the notion that your situation has a greater say than God Himself does in your life. Through the gospel message, He has spoken that you will live, even though you may die. His promise is sure, and His power is undeniable.

The life that lies ahead of you will be different from the life you had before you entered the Three Mile Valley. The goodness of God guarantees that your after will be eternally good, because you will encounter heaven someday. Until then, God is also working out all of your pain for your good. He is faithfully giving everything that happens in your life a purpose. Your best days are truly ahead of you.

Your abundantly-ever-after has already begun! Your human mind can only imagine all that God will do through the Three Mile Valley you walk. It will be worth all the sleepless nights and disappointing days! The book of James tells of the joy that we can experience by looking toward the after that God is authoring through our most difficult seasons:

> Consider it pure joy, my brothers and sisters, whenever you face trials of many kinds, because you know that the testing of your faith produces perseverance. Let perseverance finish its work so that you may be mature and complete, not lacking anything.
> —*James 1:2–4* (NIV)

As you suffer well and let perseverance finish its work, God adds maturity through your season of subtraction. With poetic power, God uses the very things that pull us apart now as tools that complete us in the end. What was meant to tear you down, God uses to grow you up. This is a good thing, because mature followers of Jesus Christ add strength to the rest of the family of God.

I have no idea what the Lord is going to do specifically through your pain. However, I can say with all confidence that it will be good!

WORKBOOK

Chapter 16 Questions

Question: How has life subtracted from you in your current suffering? How have you seen God add to you in this season?

_____

_____

_____

_____

_____

_____

_____

_____

_____

_____

_____

Question: How does an abundant life differ from a happy life?

_____

_____

_____

_____

_____

_____

_____

_____

_____

_____

_____

Action: Take some time to journal a few ways that you are allowing your circumstances to inhibit the abundant life Jesus offers you. What would it look like for you to look beyond your circumstances and trust Jesus more completely?

Chapter Sixteen Notes

THIRD MILE RECAP

Remember,
There Is Always an After

Watching God make it all right is key to conquering the third mile of the Three Mile Valley. This is the stretch of the valley that brings you face to face with God's ability to give purpose to all your pain. He will faithfully add to you while the suffering you experience subtracts from you. Your abundantly-ever-after begins now, and it will be completed when your soul enters heaven. Watching God make it all right is the reward for suffering well through the Three Mile Valley.

Declarations to Help You Remember That There Is More to Your Story:

- My God adds through seasons of subtraction.
- My God will take this test and turn it into a testimony.

- My God will take my mess and turn it into a message.
- Because Jesus is my champion, I will overcome.
- Because Jesus is enough, I will always have enough.
- Because Jesus is my freedom, I am no longer a slave.
- Because Jesus is my eternal hope, death is denied the final word in my story.
- My God will transform me through my pain, even if He does not transfer me out of my pain.
- My God will orchestrate an abundantly-ever-after that I can live with.

CONCLUSION

Suffer Well Until the End

As I reflect on my high school cross-country race back in Duluth, Minnesota, I am amazed at the journey God has taken me on since that brisk fall day. The valley that I climbed out of to begin that race was prophetic preparation for the multiple valleys through which I would walk later in life. The lessons of the Three Mile Valley contained in this book were also present in that long-ago race. As I ran, I learned that now was not forever. Through the agony of the multiple climbs out of the valley in the physical race, I discovered that I needed to choose wisely if I wanted to finish the race. And as I crossed the finish line, I experienced the truth that there is always an after!

No matter what life may throw at you, the Spirit of Christ inside of you is greater than the situation that surrounds you. He is your Champion who leads you in victory through each and every valley. Endeavor to suffer well through the difficult seasons of life. When you think right, do right, and watch God make it all right, you are well on your way to the rich and abundant life Jesus came to provide for you.

We should no longer be surprised by pain. Rather, we should purpose to see God's presence in our pain. In God's abundantly-ever-after, pain is repurposed and transformed into perseverance. What was lost is replaced with greater strength and maturity. God alone faithfully adds to us when seasons of subtraction take away from us.

Asking "why?" is a good question, but it is not the best question. The answer to that question will never change the circumstances that first triggered your plunge into the Three Mile Valley. And you still have to heal, regardless of what caused your pain. You still need to live, in spite of the challenge. And so, the most productive question in this situation becomes, "How?" And more specifically, *"How will I suffer well through the Three Mile Valley?"*

Our faith response to that question has the power to change everything. It's time to change the way we think about suffering. It is a part of life, and it is packed with divine purpose. When we hold fast in the promises of the One who is holding us, we are in the best place possible. (But notice that I didn't say the easiest or most comfortable place!)

The principles of the Three Mile Valley are simple to grasp, but they are not always easy to hold on to.

The First Mile: Now Is Not Forever

- What you see is not what you get. What you see is what you must get through.
- Perspective produces or prevents perseverance.

- Think right to suffer well.

The Second Mile: Cherish Your Choice

- Your response is your responsibility.
- Don't make permanent choices in temporary seasons.
- Do right to suffer well.

The Third Mile: There Is Always an After

- God adds through seasons of subtraction.
- God authors abundantly-ever-afters.
- Watch God make it all right to suffer well.

The path on which you are walking right now has already been conquered by Jesus. Press on and go forward with Him in victory over your valley.

You will make it through the Three Mile Valley.

You will emerge victorious.

You will make it, my friend, so suffer well until the end.

Blessed is the one who perseveres under trial because, having stood the test, that person will receive the crown of life that the Lord has promised to those who love him.
—James 1:12 *(NIV)*

Visit www.sufferwellbook.com for more resources and to share your *Suffer Well* story with us.

REFERENCES

Notes

1. Sarra L. Hedden, Joel Kennet, Rachel Lipari, Grace Medley, and Peter Tice. *Behavioral Health Trends in the United States: Results from the 2014 National Survey on Drug Use and Health. Substance Abuse and Mental Health Services Administration.* September 2015. https://www.samhsa.gov/data/sites/default/files/NSDUH-FRR1-2014/NSDUH-FRR1-2014.pdf.

About the Author

Dan Herod is an author, minister, husband, father, and friend. He loves spending time with his family, staying healthy through exercise, and serving on the local volunteer fire department.

His book, *Suffer Well*, is written from the depths of painful personal experience. In 2011, he and his wife suffered unimaginable loss when their beautiful thirteen-month-old daughter, Peyton, passed away unexpectedly in her sleep. Their journey through the valley of the shadow of death has left its mark on their lives. Dan regularly speaks about this experience in churches, youth groups, and conferences. He lives to help others by sharing his story.

Born and raised in St. Paul, Minnesota, Dan remains a Vikings fan to this day. He is an ordained minister with the

Assemblies of God (AG). Dan earned a BA in youth ministry and a minor in deaf culture studies from North Central University in Minneapolis, Minnesota. His service of over fifteen years in full-time student ministry has given him wonderful opportunities to serve people at the New Life Assembly of God (Plainfield, Wisconsin), the Christian Life Fellowship (Mayville, Wisconsin), and now as the Youth Alive director for the Wisconsin and Northern Michigan Ministries Network of the AG.

Dan and his family reside in central Wisconsin, where the summers are breathtakingly beautiful and the winters are so cold, they, too, take your breath away.

About Sermon To Book

SermonToBook.com began with a simple belief: that sermons should be touching lives, *not* collecting dust. That's why we turn sermons into high-quality books that are accessible to people all over the globe.

Turning your sermon series into a book exposes more people to God's Word, better equips you for counseling, accelerates future sermon prep, adds credibility to your ministry, and even helps make ends meet during tight times.

John 21:25 tells us that the world itself couldn't contain the books that would be written about the work of Jesus Christ. Our mission is to try anyway. Because in heaven, there will no longer be a need for sermons or books. Our time is now.

If God so leads you, we'd love to work with you on your sermon or sermon series.

Visit www.sermontobook.com to learn more.

Made in the USA
Middletown, DE
18 August 2019